Contents

Foreword

Sayings are interesting in that they help us describe different situations or people. Some situations are hard to explain and by using a certain phrase another person will know exactly what you mean. I remember when I was at school, we would have spent the whole lunchtime thinking of different things to say to each other. If you heard a new saying at home you couldn't wait to get using it on someone in school to impress the others. Everyone would have been 'in stitches laughin'.

The main inspiration for this book came a few years ago when I read a book called *'Speakin' Norn Iron'* written by my good friend and well known author Doreen McBride, it was absolutely hilarious. I couldn't put it down and it really got me thinking. Many of our sayings may have been passed down through generations and I think it's important that these are documented because there is the possibility they could be lost.

There is no hiding the fact we, as nation, have always had a huge fascination with sayings, especially in Ireland. There is not a day goes by that we aren't insulted in some way or another by some our friends. In many cases the insults or threats may sound bad to some people in other countries but those within Ireland have learned take them lightly. That's what makes us unique and we know how to have the craic. You can usually get a good measure of where the boundaries are in conversation by how far you can push someone with such sayings. It helps us understand people's personalities a lot quicker, striking many new friendships in the process.

There are a couple of sayings which I believe to be very important to remember in everyday life. When out driving always 'keep 'er between the hedges'. In business, never 'bite off more than ye can chew'. When out shopping never 'pay through the nose for somethin'. If you are going out with someone 'never show yer hand.' If you're going to a party always 'be the first there an' the last to leave.' But the most important thing to remember in life is that 'ye only live once'.

Hopefully there are lots of new sayings which you have not heard before and you will be able to use them with your friends and family. It has been an absolute pleasure writing this book and I have thoroughly enjoyed every minute of it. Some might say that 'ye couldn't bate it with a big stick!'

About the Author

I was born and reared in the parish of Annaclone in the townland of Tullyorior. Much of my childhood was spent at my neighbour's Paddy Joe McClory. It was here that I heard the numerous sayings and expressions which make up the bulk of this book. You could guarantee that in every conversation with Paddy there would be some sort of saying thrown into it. Sometimes it took me a while to work out what some of them meant but when I did I would have spent the rest of the day laughing to myself.

My school days began at St. Mary's Primary School, Banbridge and then it was on to St. Colman's College, Newry where I spent many happy days. The boys loved to slag each other off in school and this is where the vast majority of the 'insults' chapter came from. As many of my friends came from different parts of the country it was interesting to hear the different versions of sayings they used.

One of the main reasons I decided to write my own book was that when I was in Primary Seven, I was diagnosed with dyslexia and had to receive help to improve it. I refused to let it hold me back though and was determined to overcome it.

In 2009, I joined the Annaclone Historical Society and I began to take photographs for a local history book which they were publishing. I also helped out with the design of the book and wrote some articles for it. It's funny because I never had any interest in history at school but I found local history fascinating. The book was printed in November 2010 and copies have been sold all over the world.

The following year I helped co-write a ghost story book about County Down something from which I got a lot of satisfaction. I designed it myself and it was a major success.

From proof reading the other books and beginning to write articles I found that my reading skills were greatly improving. I was starting to use 'bigger words' which I would never have dreamt of using before. I even amazed myself at times as I was starting to read books from cover to cover something that I wouldn't have done as a child. This stemmed from the fact that I wasn't a good reader and found books very daunting. I couldn't help but notice some of the people that were, writing books especially celebrities, and I thought to myself if they can do it then anyone can. My new found confidence along with my life-long interest in sayings has led me to publish this book.

I have tried to cover a wide range of sayings which we use in everyday life. Most people may not have realised before reading this book the sheer number of sayings that there are and how often we use them in everyday conversation. There were obviously many sayings which I couldn't include as they were just too crude but please don't take any of the sayings which I have included the wrong way. They are not meant to offend anyone, but only to be laughed at.

I have written the expressions exactly as they would be spoken wherever possible. Our language and "slang" will continue to grow, before, during and after the publication of this book, so I hope it inspires this to continue.

Acknowledgements

The first person I want to mention is my partner in crime, Ann Marie Higgins who has been my girlfriend for a number of years for my sins. I suppose she's not the worst but she'll have to do 'til somethin' else comes along. It's hard to do with 'er an' hard to do without 'er. I wear the trousers in our relationship but she just tells me which ones to wear. If she is tired or hungry she's like a pishmire and to be avoided at all costs. She would sleep the clock round but gets up for a wee while every day. If 'er looks could kill I'd be dead years ago.

I have to give credit where credit is due to Paddy Joe McClory because without him there would be much in this book. He comes out with some big ones. There isn't a fart in the country that he doesn't know about and he's always askin' if there's anythin' fresh with ye. He does everythin' arse about face but always says there is a neck in doin' it. He has an awful sweet tooth and he likes to tell ye things on the QT. Half the country knows him and the other half want to get to know him.

His brother Thomas (Tam) McClory has got the name of an early riser but he would lie all day. He always has that much to do 'round the farm he doesn't know whether he's comin' or goin'. The way he moves around though he's like an ole woman with a straw arse. What he doesn't know about football isn't worth knowin' and he has probably forgot more than I'll ever know.

I must mention my mother and father Michael & Kathleen Wallace who made the mistake of havin' me. Dad always calls a spade a spade and if I could harrow what he has ploughed I'd be doin' well. A word of warnin' though if he ever offers you tea don't take it because he makes it that strong ye could stand on it. Kathleen has always told me to look after the pennies an' the pounds will look after themselves but I told 'er there's no point because ye can't take it with ye. Anytime she lends me money I always promise to give it back to 'er but it's more a case of live horse an' ye'll get grass. She always says to me show yer company an' I will tell ye are.

The illustrations for this book were drawn by Judith Henning and they aren't bad like but I could do better myself. She comes across as a very level headed person for 'er age and she'll not get lost anyway. She lives life to the full but she is just right because ye only live once. She's not a bad girl though, when she's sleepin' that is.

I had a few people read over the book before it went to print because I probably left out the half of it. I was fortunate enough to get the Banbridge author Doreen McBride to run 'er eye over it. She's the sort of person that would pul' ye out of a hole or wouldn't see ye stuck. What ye see is what ye get with 'er. There's no doubt about it she knows 'er stuff when it comes to writin' books and she knows the score when it comes to local language.

Gary Buchanan (AKA Bucky or Bee) also read it and made a complete haims of it. What can I say about Gary only that ye couldn't like him if ye reared him and he wouldn't spend Christmas. He would need rubbed out an' drew out again. He's the sort of fella that he wouldn't know if a dog bite him and there's more brains in a false face. In fairness though he has a whole lot of strings til' his bow and he is worth his weight in gold.

Fiona McKelvey proof read the book as well but she was as slow as a wet week. She's one of those people that have their head screwed on an' wouldn't be at a hole there was no mouse it. She'll be some pup when 'er tail grows though there's no doubt about that. One of 'er only downfalls would be that if ye took 'er outa the town she'd be lost.

The last person I would like to thank is Brian Monaghan for doin' nothin' at all. I asked him to read the book but he never bothered his arse. As a friend though he's always there when I need him and even when ye don't, he's still there. He would be late for his own funeral and he stands out like a sore thumb. Brian would go to the openin' of a letter and he spends money like water. He could talk the leg off a stool and definitely has the gift of the gab.

She has a lot of baggage with her.

Chapter 1

Birds & Animal Sayings

Two hands higher than a duck

It's like water off a duck's back.	*Something which does not last long.*
It's like a sittin' duck.	*An easy target or victim.*
He wouldn't say boo to a goose.	*A timid or an exceptionally quiet person.*
I got it straight from the horse's mouth.	*To get information first hand or direct from the source.*
It's a bad hen that does not scratch for itself.	*You have to learn to be independent.*
Ye can't expect a big egg from a wee hen.	*Don't expect a small person to do something extraordinary.*
That child is as wild as a March hare.	*A child who is unruly / badly behaved.*
I was as proud as a peacock.	*To be pleased with yourself.*
A dog is a man's best friend.	*A dog is a faithful companion.*
That'll put the cat among the pigeons.	*That will cause trouble or upset others.*
He's let the cat outa the bag.	*To inform others of a secret.*
Like a rat up a drainpipe.	*A fast mover.*
Ye can't run with the hare an' hunt with the hounds.	*You can't support both sides of a dispute.*
Who is she? The cat's mother?	*When you refer to a girl as 'she' instead of calling them by their Christian name. A mother cat is known as a 'she'.*

Most of the time a dog's bark is worse than its bite.	*Issuing exaggerated threats often unmatched by actions.*
If that happens we'll be on the pig's back.	*To be happy / content with your life or to be in fine form.*
I knew that I could smell a rat somewhere.	*You realised that something was suspicious.*
You're about two hands higher than a duck.	*An exceptionally small person.*
It'll only take two shakes of a lamb's tail.	*Something that won't take very long to do.*
They'd sit there 'til the cows come home.	*To sit in the same place for a long time.*
Don't put the kart before the horse.	*Don't do things in the wrong order.*
That person's been runnin' about all day like a headless chicken.	*Running around in a panic and not knowing what you should be doing.*
Who has ruffled yer feathers?	*Who has upset you?*
Ye look like an owl lookin' outa an ivy bush.	*You need to brush or cut your hair.*
What do ye expect from a pig only a grunt?	*That's all you can expect from him / her.*
Those who sleep with dogs rise with fleas.	*You need to be cautious about the company you keep because you could get a bad reputation.*

It's not all about the dog; it's about the fight in the dog.

Determination it is often more important than size, strength or ability.

There's life in the ole dog yet.

Describes an elderly person who does something that no one expects them to do.

Ye can't teach an ole dog new tricks.

It's difficult to teach an older person a way of doing something where they have done it the same way for years.

I'm as happy as a pig in shite.

A happy and carefree person.

As the big hound is, so will the pup be.

Like father, like son.

It was like showin' a red sheet to a bull.

Someone has seen something which has angered them.

You're like a duck with the childer all comin' after ye.

Ducks always have their offspring coming walking in a line behind them.

Better to drink milk than eat the cow.

If you do away with something completely then you cannot avail of the benefits you gained from it.

Better to lose the saddle than the horse.

It is better to lose something small than to lose a major item.

Would a cat sop milk? Would a bear shite in the woods?

A rhetorical question in response to a question where the answer is an emphatic yes.

As rough as a badger's arse.	*A very untidy looking person who takes no care of themselves. It can also mean to have a bad hang over from indulgence in alcohol or other substances.*
Ye can lead a horse to water, but ye can't make it drink it.	*You can give someone the opportunity to do something, but you can't make anyone do anything.*
The childer were jumpin' about like monkeys.	*Energetic children.*
You're a dark horse in the competition.	*Used to describe a person or team when there is little known about their capabilities.*
When the cat is away, the mice will play.	*Those people whose behaviour is strictly controlled, but who tend to go over the top when authority is not around.*
They were smilin' like a Cheshire cat.	*To grin or smile broadly.*
What's wrong has the cat got yer tongue?	*Why are you so quiet?*
Let the dog see the hare.	*To show someone the reward so that they will try to win*
A dog / elephant never forgets.	*Whatever you have taught a dog or an elephant it will never forget.*

There's a black sheep in every flock.

There is someone in every family who is bad or appears to be the odd one out in terms of dress, personality or actions.

I was sent on a wild goose chase.

To be sent in a totally different direction to the place where you wanted to go.

You're like a pig goin' to hock.

Someone who is stubborn and they have their own idea on how to do something.

Curiosity killed the cat.

Being inquisitive could lead you dangerous situations.

Can pigs fly?

There is absolutely no chance of something happening.

As sure as an eye on a goat.

Anything which is 100% certain.

The birds have all flown the nest.

Your family have left the home perhaps through emigration or marriage.

Never ask a fox to mind the hens.

Don't leave a person who cannot be trusted to do anything.

Ye may just let the hare sit for now.

Just wait and see what happens before you do anything.

A nod is as good as a wink to a blind donkey.

It doesn't matter what you do.

Never while pussy is a cat.	*You have no chance of doing something.*
The cat that got the cream.	*A person who is extremely happy because they have got what they wanted.*
The ole dog for the hard road and the pup for the pad / path.	*A father who has had a much harder life than his son.*
Hol' yer horses! Ye may hauld on a minute!	*Stop what you are doing.*
Why keep a dog an' bark yourself?	*Why would you do something yourself when you already pay someone else to do it for you?*
You've the right stable but the wrong horse.	*Someone calls you by the wrong name, but it is actually the name of another person.*
Might as well be hanged for a sheep as for a lamb.	*Being aware an action will bring severe consequences then doing something even worse as the consequence is still the same.*
A bird in the hand is worth two in the bush.	*Having one bird it's better than taking a risk in an attempt to catch two.*
As the crow flies.	*The measure of a straight distance between two points.*
It's that small that ye couldn't swing a cat in it.	*A small and cramped space.*

Wipin' the plate with the cat's tail

Ye'll be some pup when yer tail grows.	*You will be better at that in the future.*
Every dog has its day.	*Eventually a good thing will happen to you.*
He ran away like a mountain goat.	*He disappeared quickly.*
They took til' it like a calf til' a teat.	*They liked it immediately.*
I was sweatin' like a pig.	*Sweating excessively.*
Lyin' open like a pig's mouth.	*Something which is ripped or torn.*
There are many ways of chokin' a dog forby butter.	*There are many ways in which you get what you want through bribery.*
She wipes the plate with the cat's tail.	*She's very unhygienic.*

The beak of the goose is no longer than the gander.	*Men and women are equal.*
A dog with two homes is never any good.	*A dog who doesn't stay at home is not loyal to their owner.*
They're like hen's teeth.	*Very rare or near impossible to find.*
They're runnin' about like a scalded cat.	*To be rushing around in a panic.*
I'm away to see a man about a dog.	*Used to excuse yourself for an unspecified reason that you do not wish to disclose.*
One swallow never made a summer.	*To advise someone not to get too over excited because even though a couple of things have happened, there is still a long way to go.*
Don't count yer chickens before they hatch.	*Don't count on something happening before it actually does because you can never 100% sure that it will.*
Fine feathers make a fine bird.	*Nice clothes and cosmetics can make people look beasutiful.*
I'm still killin' the odd rat.	*I am still doing the occasional job now and again.*
A little birdie told me that.	*I heard something either as gossip or a rumour.*

Chapter 2
Commonly Used Phrases

Carryin' the whole world on your shoulders

I'd need to cut myself in two / half.	*Many people require your help and it is difficult to do everything.*
Ok then, good bye and God bless!	*Have a safe journey and may God look after you on your way.*
Now is yer chance to shine.	*Now's the time to use your skills to the best of your ability and show how good you are at something.*
He dropped a bombshell on us.	*To announce something that changes a situation drastically or unexpectedly.*
Whatever ye can do I can do better.	*Anything someone else can do, you can do it better.*
I need all the luck I can get.	*You realise that you will need a lot of luck to complete a task.*
Now we'll see what yer made of.	*We'll see how you cope under pressure.*
That'll be a hard pill to swallow.	*That's hard to accept.*
I had ma mind set on gettin' it.	*I really want that particular item for a long period of time.*
You're like a man on a mission.	*You look very determined to complete a task.*
I've turned over a new page / leaf.	*I am a reformed individual.*

Everythin' is out in the open now.	*When a situation or secret becomes publicly known.*
Yer guess is as good as mine.	*You do not know the answer.*
I'm tryin' to think aloud at the minute.	*I am speaking my thoughts out aloud so that others can hear what I am thinking.*
Always treat someone the way ye'd like to be treated yourself.	*Treat other people the way you would like them to treat you.*
If ye dig a grave for others ye might fall into it yourself.	*If you set a trap you could end up falling into it yourself.*
I need to iron out a few things.	*I need to sort things out.*
That'll come back to bite him in the arse / come back to haunt him.	*That action will affect him later.*
Ye wouldn't put yourself out anyway / ye wouldn't go outa yer way.	*You won't help someone.*
The alarm bells began to ring in my head.	*I realised something was wrong.*
I couldn't have done it or said it any better myself.	*I have nothing further to add.*
Someone needs to take them down a peg or two.	*Someone needs to humiliate them.*
They'll be goin' through it with a fine tooth comb.	*They will look in great detail for any mistakes.*

Even the look of it would put ye off.	*It looks scary or disgusting.*
I'll paddle ma own canoe from now on.	*I will do things for myself without help.*
They're away in 'nother world / in a wee world of their own.	*They're thinking about other things.*
That's just what the doctor ordered.	*That's exactly what was needed.*
Ye can watch a thief but ye can't watch a liar.	*It's difficult to tell when someone is lying.*
Early to bed, early to rise makes a man fit, healthy and wise.	*Going to bed and waking up early is good for success.*
It was good to get it off my chest.	*It was good to criticize or make a complaint.*
That person gives me the creeps!	*You don't like a certain person or they scare you.*
We need to get to the root of the problem.	*We need to get to the original source of a problem.*
I was saved by the bell / the whistle.	*I was saved by a last minute intervention.*
It's only a bit of a blip.	*It's a small problem or glitch.*
You're easily amused.	*You find the silliest things funny.*
I'm always shifted from pillar to post.	*I'm continuously moved around.*

He carries the whole world on his shoulders.

He has many problems / he tends to worry things.

You're just beatin' yourself up over nothin'.

You're worrying about trivial things.

Ye couldn't do right for doin' wrong.

You can't seem to get anything right no matter what you do.

I'll take it with open arms.

I will be more than glad to accept it.

It's a huge weight lifted off my shoulders.

A feeling of great relief.

There's another one to add to my collection.

When you already have a large quantity of similar items, and someone gives you another.

He jumped before he was pushed.

Someone leaves a job before they are forced to.

I'll have to show ye the ropes.

I'll teach you how to do it.

He's on eggs shells at the minute.

He is very nervous or anxious.

Ye haven't experienced the big bad world yet.

You don't realise how difficult and challenging life can be.

Finder's keepers, loser's weepers.

If you found something valuable you should be allowed to keep it because you found it first.

The more ye look at somethin' the worse it gets.

The more you analyse the more flaws you will find.

I'm walkin' on air / I'm on cloud nine / as gay as Christmas.	*I am exuberantly happy, excited and joyful.*
It was a sorry sight.	*A regrettable and unwelcome aspect / feature or a mess.*
Ye couldn't tell the difference in them two.	*They are identical.*
Little amuses the innocent.	*It doesn't take much to keep you occupied.*
Nothin' like kickin' someone when they're down.	*To aim insult or hurt towards someone when they are in a bad position.*
Ye'll cool in the same water ye boiled in.	*You are angry now but will calm down again.*
Keep the shiny side up.	*Something which bikers say to each other as they part company, translates as 'stay safe'.*
A wee white lie.	*Small untruth.*
It'll be fallin' on deaf ears.	*A poor listener.*
You're jumpin' the gun a bit.	*You're doing things too quickly.*
Ye can choose who ye marry but ye can't choose yer family.	*You can choose your partner but you have to accept your relatives.*
You're a bad egg.	*You are evil.*

That's the shape of things to come.	*That's an indication of what things will be like in the future.*
You're well down the peckin' order.	*You are low on rank or status.*
Everythin' will be plain sailin' from 'ere on.	*Everything will be easy in the future.*
I couldn't give a damn.	*I couldn't care less.*
Ye may put it on the back burner.	*You may postpone doing something for a while.*
Wipe the slate clean.	*To put a disagreement behind you.*
That's not to be sniffed at.	*That's worth considering further.*
Ye need to nip that in the bud.	*You must stop that at an early stage.*
That rings a bell with me.	*That reminds me of something.*
Speak of the Divil.	*When a person who has just been referred to suddenly appears.*
You're stuck in the mud.	*You can't find a way out.*
We'll have to get down to the nitty-gritty.	*We will have to get down to the basics.*
I'd give my right hand for it.	*I would sacrifice a great deal for it.*

Ye should keep yer feet on the ground.	*You mustn't get carried away.*
He read him the royal act.	*He scolded him severely.*
That's part an' parcel of it.	*That's all about it.*
It'll be touch an' go.	*It's risky.*
He's been fed off the land.	*He's the best fed man in the country.*
It's only history repeatin' itself.	*When something happens again to the same person / family which has happened before.*
I just lost the rag.	*I was furious.*
They'll turn the other cheek to it.	*They will ignore it.*
Ye may keep me posted.	*You may keep me informed.*
They're startin' to dig their heels in.	*They are beginning to be stubborn.*
I just got through by the skin of my teeth.	*I finished by the narrowest of margins.*
He's an ordinary run of the mill fella or an ordinary 5 8".	*He is a normal man or advantage height.*
We ran outa steam.	*We didn't have the energy to finish.*
I had a bit of a senior moment there.	*I forgot about something or become confused.*

A house wife's work is never endin'.

A house wife is always busy.

How long is a piece of string?

It's impossible to say how long something will take.

One half of the world doesn't know how the other half lives.

You don't realise how many luxuries or holidays someone else has while you work hard.

Were ye born in a hospital with swingin' doors?

Can you not close doors after you?

You're only as old as ye feel.

You might be an elderly person but you might feel a lot younger than you look.

The person that has never made a mistake hasn't been born yet.

Everyone makes mistakes.

All in a day's work.

It was no trouble to you.

Many hands make light work.

Many people helping out completes a job quickly.

I don't want to step on anyone's toes.

I don't want to upset anyone.

That took the sting out of it.

To slightly improve a situation that is unpleasant.

We've never really seen eye to eye.

We have never agreed.

Ye never know what ye can do 'til ye try.

If you do not try something out it is impossible to tell how good or bad you are at it.

It'll be a different story when the shoe is on the other foot.	*If things were turned around and they were the opposite of what they were originally.*
I'll do this first just to test the water.	*I will try this first to see what happens.*
They've ants in their pants.	*They cannot stay in the same place for any length of time.*
He's just settin' himself up for a great fall.	*A person who does lots of things which will ultimately end up going wrong for them.*
She has a bun in the oven.	*A woman who is pregnant.*
It never rains but it pours.	*Things don't usually happen for a while and then everything seems to happen at once.*
Ye could have cut the tension between them with a knife.	*There was a lot of tension in the room.*
I'll give them a piece of my mind.	*I will tell them my true feelings.*
That'll put that to bed now.	*That will put an end to it.*
He's punchin' above his weight.	*He is doing more than is expected of him.*
It's as broad as it is long.	*It is the same no matter what way you look at it.*
We'll have to get the ball rollin'.	*We will have to get started on the task.*

I took cold feet.	*I became scared and didn't proceed with something.*
Ye'll not fall out with yer company anyway.	*You're alone in a room or field, church, etc.*
They'll probably brow beat ye into doin' it.	*They will force you to do something which you may not have wanted to do.*
Guard it with yer life.	*Look after something carefully.*
There's no point on gettin' hung up on that.	*There is no point in becoming annoyed.*
That person likes to sit on the fence.	*Those people do not like to take sides or have an opinion.*
I've a lump in my throat.	*I am feeling emotional.*
Enjoy it while it lasts.	*Make the most of it.*
I'll have to draw the line.	*I will have to set a limit (often between what one will and will not tolerate.)*
There are no half measures with him anyway.	*A person who puts his heart and soul into things.*
To go that extra mile.	*To try harder to please someone or to get a task done correctly.*
It's all a bit cloudy at the minute.	*It is unclear at present.*

They like to sit on the fence

Everythin' is up in the air at the moment.	*No one knows what is happening.*
That takes the biscuit.	*That is astonishing.*
I won't lose any sleep over it.	*I will not worry about it.*
That's all in the pipeline.	*It will be completed soon.*
To give someone the heads up.	*To inform someone about what is going on in a particular situation.*
I haven't seen ye in a month of Sundays.	*I haven't seen you for in a long time.*
Try walkin' a mile in my boots / shoes.	*Try to imagine what life would be like if you were in my position*

It has never happened to me before but there's always a first time!	*Even though something has not happened to you before it does not mean you can rule out the possibility of it happening for the first time.*
Off the beaten track.	*To do something which you are not use to.*
He's always on my case / on my back.	*He is constantly harassing me.*
They must have slipped the net.	*They must have been overlooked.*
It's a small world.	*When you meet someone who you haven't seen for years in the most unlikely of places.*
Ye never know what could happen if ye play yer cards right.	*Things may work in your favour if you do things in a certain way.*
Call a spade a spade.	*To describe something / someone exactly as it should be described or to put it bluntly.*
I tell a lie!	*I've realised that I've said something incorrect.*
Ye may sling yer hook.	*Clear off.*
He has his finger in a lot of pies.	*Someone who is involved in many different things.*
The jury is out on that one.	*It hasn't been decided.*

You're funny! Funny lookin'!	*Someone who tries to be funny but they are not funny at all.*
The writin' is on the wall.	*It's just a matter of time until it happens.*
They'll have the whole thing sewn up.	*It has already been decided.*
Ye'd be the worst in the world.	*Everyone would hate you.*
Pull one outa the bag.	*To do something spectacular.*
I'm tryin' to find my feet.	*I am trying to become more confident.*
That put ye in yer box.	*To let someone know where they stand.*
Keep yer mouth closed or you'll put yer foot in it.	*Be careful what you say because it could get you into trouble.*
Ye may put yer head on the block.	*You are going to take a risk.*
He's livin' on the edge.	*He's in an uncertain situation.*
God helps him who helps himself.	*God helps those who make an effort.*
There must be two moons in the sky.	*That is unbelievable.*
Nothin' is ever as bad as it seems.	*Imagination makes things appear worse.*

It's not easy pleasin' everyone or keepin' everyone happy.	*Anytime you plan an event there will be someone who isn't happy as they will have their own opinion.*
A lie travels further than the truth.	*Rumours tend to travel fast.*
God only knows.	*No ones knows what happened.*

Illness

I was as sick as a dog.	*Vomiting all over the place.*
My stomach is churnin' / turnin'.	*I feel sick.*
Ye look like a corpse.	*Looking ill.*
I feel as if I've one foot in the grave.	*I feel like I am going to die.*
She took a wee turn.	*She became ill suddenly.*
Ye look like death warmed up.	*To be quite pale or to look very ill.*
I'm feelin' a bit under the weather.	*To feel unwell.*
It came outa of me as quick as it went in.	*When you have diarrhoea and it's coming out of you as quick as you ate it.*
It was comin' outa me at both ends.	*When you have vomiting and diarrhoea at the same time.*

Spoilt

It's their way or no way.	*Those who insist on getting their own way.*
He'd take everythin' and give nothin'.	*He asks for favours but doesn't return them.*
It's about time ye started to milk yer own goat.	*You should be out earning your own money instead of taking money off others.*
He gets fed like a King.	*A person who is fed on the best food money can buy and in large quantities.*
I've everythin' under the sun.	*I have everything I want.*
He's always took by the hand.	*He always gets things given to him.*
Set in their ways.	*People who do not like change.*
Ah has the big child threw his dummy out?	*Someone who has become annoyed over something silly.*
It's about time ye stood on yer own two feet.	*To be independent and provide for yourself.*
He's wrapped in cotton wool.	*Someone who is carefully protected; kept out of harm's way.*
They get everythin' handed to them.	*Those who do very little for themselves and receive lots of things free of charge.*

The big child has threw his dummy out

Giving orders

Ye may stop while you're ahead.

You should stop doing something that is rewarding but risky before something bad happens.

As long as you're under my roof, ye'll live under my rules.

When you are in my house you will abide by my rules / wishes.

What did yer last slave die of?

A person who is demanding or who gives a lot of orders to other people instead of doing anything for themselves.

Tiredness

I slept like a log last night.

I slept soundly.

I'm very far through.	*I am totally exhausted.*
I'm that tired that I'd sleep on a washin' line.	*People say this to emphasise how tired they are that they could sleep anywhere.*
They're out for the count / they were like a sleepin' baby.	*They are in a deep sleep.*
I'm completely knackered.	*I am feeling very tired.*
I'd need to get my batteries re-charged.	*I need to go lie down and take a rest as I am tired.*
I'm that tired that I could sleep for a week.	*I am exhausted and could sleep for a very long time.*
I'm so tired that I'm dead on my feet.	*I have no energy and feel lifeless.*

Death

He has kicked the bucket.	*He has died.*
She got away quick.	*She died suddenly.*
God always seems to take the good ones.	*Good people always seem to die young.*
Another clean shirt will do ma.	*It won't be long until I am dead.*
Dead men tell no lies.	*Dead people will not disclose any secrets.*
'ere the day, gone the'mara.	*You could be living today but you could be dead the following day.*

Never speak ill of the dead.	*Don't speak bad of the dead.*
There was a good turnout at the funeral.	*A huge crowd attended the funeral.*
Every day is a day nearer the grave.	*Each day brings you closer to your death.*
Ye shouldn't talk about the dead.	*It is disrespectful to speak badly of the death.*
He's on his last legs.	*Someone who is about to die.*
It'll not be long 'til we're under the sowd.	*It won't be long until we are dead and buried.*
If its praise ye want, die.	*You receive more praise when you are dead.*
They're just waitin' on 'er now.	*They are expecting her to die.*

I feel like I have one foot in the grave

Chapter 3
The
Countryside

Do you think I came up the River Bann in a bubble?

It was no bigger than a sparrow's fart.	*It is tiny or non-existent.*
I juked out to see who was goin' past.	*I looked outside.*
It's like the wheelbarrow; it's in front of ye.	*Don't worry because it'll happen in the future.*
I could have been killed stone dead.	*I could have been killed.*
Take 'er handy.	*Drive the car carefully.*
I'm away 'ere to make ma water.	*I am going to urinate.*
Hell slap it up ye!	*To say that someone deserved it.*
That'll be a bit of a slap in the mouth for ye!	*That will be a nasty shock.*
I'll give ye a penny for yer thoughts.	*What are you thinking about?*
How's she cuttin'?	*How are things?*
How's the form?	*How are you?*
Well, what are ye at this weather?	*What have you been doing recently?*
They're tryin' to cut a quare dash.	*They are showing off.*
It's just like our house, there's nothin' in it.	*This describes two things which are close together.*

You're great at readin' up the country.

You are good at speaking badly of everyone.

Stop cluddin' stones!

Stop throwing stones.

He's away gallivantin' tonight.

He's out partying / socialising.

Not a word of it.

You don't believe what someone is telling you.

Sure it'll be a bit of value anyway if nothin' else.

It should be a bit of fun.

Ye couldn't beat it with a big stick.

You couldn't get much better.

Did ye get yer ears moved back?

You got your hair cut recently.

Ah I'm sure that would fatten ye!

A present or money that was given to you which you don't think much of it.

I'll have a gander at that.

I will take a good look.

Do ye think I was reared under a bowl?

Do you think I am stupid and I don't know anything?

Catch a grip of yourself.

Don't be silly / don't be stupid.

Watch yer house!

Look out!

They're all splittin' with the same hatchet.

They are all of the same opinion.

I don't know what you're crowin' about.

I don't know why you are boosting.

There ye are now!   *That is the end of that!*

Let's face it.   *Let's be realistic.*

That's a holy tarra.   *That is terrible.*

Ye must have little to be at.   *You must have nothing else to do.*

Right! Look after yourself.   *Good bye and be careful.*

Do ye want a hand with that?   *Do you would any help?*

I was covered in muck from head to toe.   *I was filthy.*

Ye couldn't hear yer ears.   *It was very noisy.*

That's a cock an' bull story.   *That is a lot of rubbish.*

Awk would ye stop!   *That is nonsense.*

I'm at the end of my tether.   *I can't do anymore.*

If in doubt ride 'er out.   *Keep at it no matter what.*

No rest for the wicked.   *There is a lot to do.*

Keep 'er country.   *Keep listening to country music.*

I near died.   *I was shocked.*

Don't be jumpin' the gun.   *Don't jump to conclusions.*

I'm not goin' to feather his nest.   *I am not going to provide for him.*

Pressure is only for tyres.	*People might use this expression whenever someone says you must be under pressure or stressed out.*
Ye could turn it in a six pence.	*A vehicle which can be turned in a small space.*
Do ye think I came down in the last shower of rain?	*Do you think that I am stupid?*
It's like Fort Knox.	*A building which is difficult to gain access to.*
Live horse an' ye'll get grass.	*Describes a person who promises a lot of things but never comes up with anything.*
I'm not gona bother my arse.	*I am not going to do it.*
They don't make things like they used to.	*Modern items aren't as well made as old ones.*
The divil the hate.	*You are not doing much.*
It was hell for lather.	*Going at great speed.*
Awk I was only coddin' ye.	*I was only joking.*
Well, are ye rightly?	*Are you keeping well?*
Is there anythin' fresh with ye?	*Did you hear any news lately?*
There'd be more craic at a wake.	*An event which has a poor atmosphere.*

Ye can take the lad outa the country but ye can't take the country outa the lad.	*You can take a person into the town but they will still stay the same as they were in the country.*
I wouldn't see ye stuck.	*I would guarantee to help you.*
Ye wouldn't know who might take the door.	*You could be surprised who might visit.*
He looked at ma as if I had horns!	*Refers to someone who looks at you with a confused look on their face.*
Right. Good Luck!	*Good Bye!*
My house is full of this, that an' the other.	*My house is full of everything and anything.*
It's a quare skelp to yonder.	*That would be quite a distance away.*
They'll drag ye into the gutters.	*Bad influence can have a bad influence on you.*
I was lyin' low last night.	*I didn't do anything the last night.*
The craic was 90.	*It was great fun.*
Oh boys a dear, that beats it all.	*That is shocking.*
Do ye think I came up the River Bann in a bubble?	*Do you think I'm stupid?*
They're too long in the tooth to believe that.	*They will not be easily fooled.*

We've the back broke anyway.	*We've most of the job done.*
I'm none the wiser.	*I still don't understand what you are talking about.*
What neck of the woods are ye from?	*Where do you live?*
There's a knack in doin' it.	*There is an easy way to do things.*
He was walkin' in the middle of the road like Brown's cows.	*He walks down the middle of the road.*
I ran outa road.	*I put my car off the road or over the hedge.*
Outa the fryin' pan an' into the fire.	*Jumping from one bad situation to another.*
On yer feet an' on the street.	*Get up we are leaving now.*
I'll do that in the heel of the evenin'.	*I will do that late in the day.*
It's only a stone throw away	*It's nearby.*
They must pay more road tax than me.	*They take up most of the road.*
Back in my day there was none of that.	*When I was younger things were different.*
That's wild altogether.	*That is hard to believe.*
I see ye have got help.	*Usually said to those who have just had a baby.*

Ye need red out or swept out.	*Said to someone who has done an extremely fool fart.*
That wouldn't cut butter.	*Describes anythin' which is not sharp.*

Farmer's talk

It's bad whenever ye arrive home, with yer partner and yer brother goes for the bale lift to get 'er wrapped.	*Your family think that your partner is overweight.*
Someone must have opened the wrappin' on the bale lately because they've blew out.	*They have gained a lot of weight lately.*
He's a slippers farmer.	*His income comes from renting his land not farming it.*
Ye couldn't turn them with the pitch fork.	*You couldn't change their minds.*
He's feedin' the cows on the long acre.	*Allowing cows to graze on the roadside grass.*
It's not easy for the small farmer.	*Life can be difficult for some people.*
Every cock crows loudly in his own farmyard but not so loudly in anyone else's.	*It is easy to be assertive in your own environment but difficult elsewhere.*
A farmer's work is never done.	*Farmer's have work to do seven days a week.*

If the moisture is right, cut all night!	*If the conditions are right keep on harvesting.*
Ye wouldn't know to step back from the trough / table.	*A person who is overweight and greedy.*
That cow wouldn't cream yer tea.	*The cow has no milk.*
He fell aff him like chaff.	*Refers to a player who ran into another player during a football match and came off the worst.*
Give us a bit of that cow.	*Pass the milk.*
You're like an ole woman with a straw arse.	*You resemble like an old stiff woman.*
His t-shirt is that big, that it would do for a cover for a car trailer.	*He is wearing a really large t-shirt.*
There's a person that wasn't beat away from the trough anyway.	*Those people who are overfed.*
He's well wintered.	*This is a phrase which farmers use to describe a beast that has fattened up well over the wintertime. A person who has put on a lot of weight.*
She looks like she has been trailed through a hedge back ways.	*She looks untidy.*
I could lick meal off yer head.	*I am taller than you!*

Ye'd think that ye tied 'er on behind the tractor an' trailed 'er after ye.	*She is ugly.*
There wouldn't be what would wipe yer arse or fill the wheelbarrow on that field.	*A field with very little grass on it.*
It was up an' down like a purta picker.	*It was constantly moving up and down.*
If she's not a Deere she'll not be 'ere.	*If the tractor is not a John Deere you don't want it.*
Nothin' runs like a Deere.	*Nothing runs like a John Deere tractor.*
If ye see a Deere just give 'er another gear.	*If you see a John Deere tractor on the road just go past it.*
Now we're suckin' diesel.	*Things are starting to get better.*
If ye could harrow, what I've ploughed.	*If you could do what I have already done in my life it would be an achievement.*
If ye reaped what I've sowed, I'll shake yer hand.	*If you do what I have done I'll congratulate you.*
Ye can't whistle an' chew meal at the same.	*Multitasking is difficult.*
If I like the sow I like 'er litter.	*If you like the parents you will like their children.*
Thon thing has some end on it.	*A beast which has a muscular rear end.*

There's no need to fear the wind if yer haystacks are tied down.	*Don't fear something if you are prepared for it.*
Ye needa cut the meal off 'er.	*A girl is getting too fat and could do with less food.*
If ye don't want flour on yer shoes, don't go to the mill.	*Don't go to a place if you know that you are going to get dirty.*
It's like tryin' to find a needle in a hay stack.	*An item that is nearly impossible to find due to everything that is around it.*
Separate the wheat from the chaff.	*Separate the good from the bad.*

Now we are suckin' diesel!

Ye'll never plough a field by turnin' it over in yer head.

You won't get anything done just by thinking about.

Truckers talk

There would be more power in a good fart.

A vehicle which has a low horse power and is incapable of pulling heavy loads.

Keep 'er low goin' through Arbow.

Be careful or watch yourself. (This saying comes from Arbow, in Tyrone which has many low bridges and you need to watch driving through it encase you hit any of them, especially in a lorry.)

Ye'll never be late in a V8.

You won't be late for a delivery, if you have a V8 engine.

If it has no V, it's not for me.

I won't drive a vehicle unless it has a V8 engine.

Ye better watch ye don't get reserved over 'round 'ere.

Often said whenever a group of people are talking about their driving experiences.

Keep 'er between the hedges / the greenery.

Don't put the car off the road.

Three steps to heaven.

There are three steps into the lorry and when you go up then you would think that you're in heaven.

If ye cannae hol' 'er ye have te rol' er.	*If you can't hold your vehicle on the road you might end up rolling or tipping it over.*
That's a 10:4 Roger!	*That's fine or talk to you soon.*
I've reserved further than you've drove / I've pushed the spare wheel further than you've drove.	*I am a better driver than you and I have had more driving experience.*
That's not ill Magill.	*That is great news.*
Ye couldn't turn it in a field.	*A vehicle which is very difficult to turn.*

Driving recklessly & the need for speed

Put the pedal to the metal.	*Go as fast as possible.*
The car took off like a bat outa hell.	*The car started off very quickly.*
We'll gather that gear up th'mara.	*The sound when a person crunches gears while driving.*
He was away like the clappers.	*He went very quickly.*
If the roads are empty give 'er plenty.	*If there are no other vehicles on the road go as fast as you can.*
I was comin' down the hill fulla' the pipe.	*I was travelling as fast as I could go.*

Ye may open that door an' let the clutch out.	*Those who drive in a low gear and use a high level of revs without changing gear.*
He was goin' down the road like Joe 90.	*He was going at high speed.*
I was cuttin' the dung outa 'er.	*I was driving recklessly.*
It went like snow off a ditch.	*It disappeared extremely quickly.*
He drove the brains outa that yoke.	*He showed no respect for his car.*
Are ye takin' this yoke for a bit of a hoke?	*Are you going to drive this car fast?*
The road turned an' I didn't.	*I had an accident on a corner.*
He's away down the road doin' 90 to the dozen.	*He is travelling at a great speed.*
If ye can't smoke 'em choke 'em.	*If you can't beat someone for speed, fill the road full of smoke so they can't see.*
Let 'er at it.	*Put the accelerator down.*
Ye wouldn't see him for dust.	*He disappeared quickly.*
Don't slack 'er 'til ye wreck 'er.	*Don't stop going fast until you crash your car.*
If in doubt, pull out!	*Don't be sit behind a slow vehicle, over take them.*

If in doubt, flat out!	*Drive the vehicle as fast as it will go.*
I'll smoke ye / blow ye aff / leave ye for dead.	*My car is much faster than yours.*
They like to take plenty of the road with 'em.	*A person who won't pull in to let you past on a road.*
Drive it like ye stole it.	*To go as fast as you can.*
Drive it like you're late for mass.	*Drive the car as if you're late.*
Ye'd think he was goin' to put a fire out.	*Someone who was travelling very fast and seem to be in a hurry.*
Keep 'er lit.	*Keep on going.*
The headlight was pushed right out of 'er.	*To travel at great speed.*
Let 'er at it / give 'er dicksy!	*Put the accelerator down.*
They were comin' like the hammers of hell.	*They were moving fast.*
Blow the cob webs outa 'er.	*Drive a vehicle at high speed.*
He's away down the road in the car like a rocket.	*To move off at high speed.*
Are ye drivin' long?	*Used whenever anyone makes a mistake while driving.*
She's away like a fart in the wind / snow off a ditch.	*To get away from somewhere quickly or in an instant.*

Describin' our vehicles

That car is a parcel of shite.	*That car is a bundle of trouble.*
Ye need the pyer.	*Usually said to someone after you have lifted something which they couldn't lift or else it could be referring to a vehicle.*
That car has more hits than the Beetles.	*A car which is covered in dents.*
I wouldn't drive that into a wall.	*I don't like that car.*
That's a quare auld yoke ye have.	*Your old car is in good condition.*
That car is goin' like a watch.	*A car that is running well.*
Don't buy it if ye can't fuel it.	*Don't buy a car if you can't afford the fuel.*
That car is completely banjaxed.	*That car is wrecked.*
That car is as dead as hector.	*The car has very little power.*
Thon thing is goin' like a bag of bottles.	*Describes a noisy car.*
Wash it anymore an' ye'll wash it away.	*Spending a long or excessive time washing something.*

Chapter 4

Comparisons

Smokin' like a chimney

Growin' like a mushroom.	*To grow rapidly.*
Two sides of the same coin.	*Two ways of seeing something.*
Sharp as the mother-in-law's tongue.	*A spiteful person.*
Rumours can spread like a wild fire.	*Rumour spread quickly.*
Up like a puff of smoke.	*Something that disappeared quickly.*
Away like a flash or sheet lightenin'.	*Something like disappeared quickly.*
Thon fella smokes like a chimney or a train.	*He is a heavy smoker.*
My hands are like ice.	*My hands are cold.*
That family is just like a set of stairs.	*There is little difference in the age or height of the children.*
You're standin' there like two policemen.	*You are standing still.*
They're like Santa Claus at Christmas.	*Everyone is looking for a particular person at the same time.*
That potato is just like soap.	*A potato with a waxy texture and doesn't taste nice.*
Cryin' like a baby.	*Crying uncontrollably.*
Stick together like glue.	*Those who support each other.*

Their garden is like a jungle.	*Their garden which is untidy and overgrown.*
Everythin' just fitted into place like a jigsaw.	*Everything fitted easily.*
They're like a fish out of water.	*Someone who is out of their depth.*
It'll go through it like a knife through butter.	*To go through something with ease.*
He has a neck on him like a Charolais bull.	*A person who has a thick / fat neck.*
She's as wide as a Mulligar heifer.	*To have a quite fat / wide back side.*
The atmosphere was electric.	*There was a huge 'buzz'.*
It was like a storm in a tea cup.	*An argument blown out of proportion.*
Growin' like a weed.	*Something which has a sudden growth sprout.*
You're like a cat on a hot tin roof.	*Someone who doesn't stay in the one place very long and is nervous or grumpy.*
Lit up like a Christmas tree / a lighthouse.	*A building with many lights turned on at the same time.*
It's like Aladdin's cave.	*A place full of desirable or valuable objects.*
Wrapped up like an onion.	*To have many layers of clothing on.*

I can read ye like a book.	*I know exactly what to expect from you because of your actions in the past.*
Round ye like a clegg.	*Someone who is a nuisance.*
Goin' like a fiddler's elbow.	*To be moving very fast in a repetitive motion.*
A smile as broad as the Shannon.	*To have huge smile on your face.*
Swelled up like a balloon.	*To have a large swelling.*
They just sink to the bottom like a stone / like a ton of bricks.	*They are not buoyant.*
Runnin' like a tap.	*Something which is flowing uncontrollably.*
You're just like a doormat, everyone walks all over ye.	*You are not assertive.*
They've that many animals in the house it's like Noah's Ark.	*Many different animals all living in the same place.*
Sleepin' like a mouse in a meal barrel.	*To be sleeping sound and full of food.*
They've an arse like a bag of washin'.	*A person with a bottom covered in cellulite or fat.*
You're like a dog 'atin' hot chips.	*Someone who eats in an unrefined manner.*
Yer standin' there like a rabbit in the headlights.	*You are shocked and motionless.*

That landscape is like a picture on a postcard.

An idyllic landscape.

The place is like a cattle market.

This place is overcrowded.

Yer hair is like a wind bush.

Your hair is a mess.

He was up like a salmon.

To leap high into the air.

They've a head like a sieve.

A very forgetful person.

Shinin' like a new shillin' / a new pin.

Extremely clean or just like new.

They're runnin' about the house like a herd of elephants.

People moving around together making a lot of noise.

Their house is like a maze.

Their house has a very confusing layout.

His hands are like sandpaper.

He has rough hands.

Those glasses are like milk bottles.

A pair of glasses with thick lenses.

They've hands on them like shovels or like Tyson. (Mike Tyson the boxer).

To have large hands.

It'll put hairs on yer chest like shot leeks.

Used to encourage young boys to eat vegetables or crusts.

They're like a bank machine.

Someone with a lot of money.

He's walks like John Wayne.

He walks with a swagger.

You're like a bull in a china shop.	*Someone who is very careless or clumsy.*
They're like calves let out for the first time.	*A group of people acting crazy for no apparent reason.*
I'm like a tin man that would need oiled.	*To have sore joints and aching all over.*
When they sing they are like a cat cryin'.	*Poor singers and those who are hard to listen to.*
Snorin' like a bog eel.	*Snoring loudly.*
They're always watchin' us like a hawk.	*To watch someone's every move.*
His head looks like a queue ball.	*A bald person who has a smooth and polished head.*
You're like the bus. Ye stop at every hole in the hedge.	*Someone who tends to stop everywhere.*
A head like a computer.	*To have an excellent memory.*
You're like the milkman ye only deliver now an' again.	*You are unreliable.*
As broad as a barn beam.	*Something which is quite wide.*
As dull as dish / ditch water.	*Someone with no personality / sour.*
As thick as thieves.	*Very close friends.*
As solid as a rock.	*Very durable.*

As white as a sheet.	*Very pale.*
As soft as a baby's bottom.	*Soft, smooth to touch.*
As hard as nails.	*A tough person.*
As hard as the road.	*If a certain person hit you it would be very hard and it would hurt you.*
As happy as Larry.	*To be very happy.*
As slow as a funeral.	*Very slow.*
As red as a beetroot.	*To be embarrassed and go red in the face or to be sun burnt.*
As stiff as a poker.	*Extremely stiff and sore. Aching from head to toe.*
As fresh as a daisy.	*Energetic and well rested.*
As old as the hills.	*Ancient or someone who is advanced in years.*
As straight as a dye.	*Anything which stays in a very straight line and never moves in any other direction.*
As yellow as a ragweed.	*Something which is yellow in colour.*
As sound as a pound.	*A very good or reliable person.*
As safe as a row of houses.	*Something which is very safe and will not move or collapse.*
As slow as a cart horse.	*A slow person.*

As blind as a bat.	*A person who has poor eyesight.*
As weak as water.	*To feel tired and you haven't got much energy.*
As plain as day / it's plain to be seen.	*It was easily understood.*
As thick as champ.	*To be stupid or bad tempered.*
As clear as day.	*Something which is clearly understood.*
As dark as the nights sky.	*A very dark object.*
As fresh as paint.	*To feel alert and not tired at all.*
As mad as a hatter.	*Crazy people.*
As black as the sole of yer boot / as black as the road / as black as the ace of spades.	*A darkly coloured item.*
As snug as a bug in a rug.	*To be very cosy.*
As grey as a rat or like a silver fox.	*A full head of grey hair.*
As dead as a door nail.	*Dead or lifeless when referring to plants / people or animals.*
As light as a kite.	*Someone who is light in weight and can be lifted easily.*
As high as kite.	*To be over excited or thrilled about something.*

As flat as a pancake.	*Something which is very flat or thin.*
As warm as wool.	*To be very warm.*
As stiff as a board.	*You feel very stiff and sore.*
As cool as a cucumber.	*Someone who doesn't panic under pressure.*
As clean as whistle.	*Something which is exceptionally clean or someone who is not involved in any illegal activity.*
As fit as a fiddle.	*To be in good health and have a high level of physical fitness.*
As sweet as whistle.	*Anything which stays in a straight line or doesn't move off course.*
As brown as a berry.	*Very brown.*
As raw as ropes.	*An ignorant person.*
Like a child with a new toy.	*Something delights you.*
Like a child in a sweetie shop.	*To be very happy and excited about the things around you making you act in a silly way.*
Like the blind leadin' the blind.	*Uninformed people showing other incapable people what to do / where to go.*
Like a lance.	*Very sharp.*

Like sardines in a tin.	*Squeezed into a confined space.*
Like two peas in a pod.	*People who are very alike.*
Like a pishmer.	*To be angry and easily frustrated.*
Like a pin cushion.	*A person who gets many needles inserted into them.*
Like watchin' paint dry.	*Extremely boring.*
Like watchin' the grass grow.	*Something that is so slow you wouldn't notice it changing.*
Like a shoot in the dark.	*Taking a chance.*
Like day an' night.	*To be totally different.*
Like a drop in the ocean.	*It is insignificant.*
Like a flash in the pan.	*It happened very quickly.*
Like chalk an' cheese.	*Two completely different people.*
Like gold dust.	*Something which is different to obtain.*
Like a pig's sty.	*Those people who live in that house have poor hygiene.*
Like a herron on a hot gridal.	*Someone or something that is constantly moving around.*
Like a spider goin' up the wall.	*To move up something at great speed.*

Chapter 5

Popular Irish Sayings

Caught between a rock an' a hard place.	*A difficult situation which may be hard to get out of.*
Speak now or forever hold yer peace.	*Say whatever you have to say now because you may not have another opportunity.*
The smaller the house, the wider the door.	*You are more than likely to be invited into a small house than a large house.*
It's all done above board.	*Something that has been completed honestly and without hiding anything from anyone else.*
Ye'll be doin' it against the grain.	*Going against the natural order of things.*
There was only a whisper or a thou in it.	*To win or lose by the narrowest of margins or by a small amount.*
That'll keep ma tickin' over for a while anyway.	*That is enough to keep me going for a short time.*
Hit him he's no relation.	*What you do to him is of no consequence to me.*
That's a totally different kettle of fish.	*That is a different matter.*
You're only cuttin' a stick to beat yourself.	*You are only going to harm yourself.*
Everythin' is in the meltin' pot.	*Things are liable to change.*

Ye'll have to grasp the nettle.	*You will have to face the problem.*
They're only tryin' to cover their own arse.	*They are attempting to protect themselves.*
The track of the nappy is not off their arse yet.	*It is not that long since the person was a child.*
Ask no questions, hear no lies.	*No queries, no untruths.*
I might have been born at night but it wasn't last night.	*I am not stupid.*
A shot a fodder.	*You are hungry.*
Jesus, Mary and Joseph.	*Usually said after a sudden scare or something has gone wrong.*
I'm headin' out to the sticks.	*I am going out into the countryside.*
It just came outa the blue.	*It happened unexpectedly.*
Ye may just cut the tail of bad luck.	*You have to accept it.*
I don't want to get off on the wrong foot with them.	*I don't want to begin by annyoing them.*
He's a dead ringer for his brother / father.	*He looks exactly like his brother / father.*
That's me back on the straight and narrow.	*That is me back to normal.*

You're not a kick in the arse off it.	*You are very close to something.*
I think I'll take a back seat from now on.	*I am not going to take responsibility anymore.*
Did ye get outa the wrong side of the bed this mornin'?	*You have a bad temper or you are grumpy for no apparent reason.*
You've shot yer bolt.	*You have blown your opportunity at something or with someone.*
I doubt you've missed the bus.	*I think you have lost an opportunity.*
Ye may knock the whole thing on the head.	*Forget about it.*
I'll talk to ye when you're better dressed.	*Usually said to someone when you are parting company with them.*
Ye'll be knockin' at the door anyway.	*You will be quite close to something.*
I was just bitin' / chappin'/ champin' at the bit.	*I couldn't wait to get started on something.*
They're a law onto themselves.	*They do whatever they like.*
I'm on the crest of a wave.	*I am feeling happy.*
Born on the wrong side of the blanket.	*Illegitimate child.*

That has never happened me anyway, 'Touch wood!'	*Knocking on wood is supposed to bring you good luck.*
Ye'll be as right as rain in the mornin'.	*You will recover quickly.*
You've shot yourself in the foot.	*You have done something that will hamper your opportunities in the future.*
Oh he'll be spittin' blood / he'll be like a spittin' bull.	*He will be very angry.*
He's only talkin' blarney.	*He is talking rubbish.*
Make sure and use plenty of elbow grease.	*Use plenty of effort and physical power.*
That boy is like an ole head on young shoulders.	*That boy is unusually sensible for his age.*
There's a hole in everythin'.	*Nothing's perfect.*
If ye scratch my back, I'll scratch yours.	*If you do something for me then I will do something for you in return.*
You're a long time dead, before you're gone.	*Be happy when you are alive because you will be dead much longer than you will be alive.*
I can't see the wood for the trees.	*I am missing the overall picture.*
He's the spittin' image of his dad.	*He looks exactly like his father.*

They call the shots 'round 'ere.	*They give the orders here.*
He has many nicks in his horn.	*Someone who has done a lot in his life.*
The storm's liftin' his thatch.	*He is going bald.*
Ye make yer own luck.	*Luck is due to effort.*
If he asked ye to jump into / put yer hand in the fire would ye do it?	*Would you do something that someone told you to do no matter how bad it was or what danger it might put you in?*
There are horses for courses.	*People have different talents.*
Jack of all trades, master of none.	*Someone who is able to do a variety of jobs but aren't particularly good at any of them.*
Ye can't start a story an' not finish it.	*Said to a person who begins to tell a story but decides not to reveal all the details.*
He has the luck of the Irish.	*He is very lucky.*
There's a time and a place for everythin'.	*Not acting in a way which is suitable for the situation.*
Tomorrow is a new day.	*Tomorrow offers a new opportunity to do things.*
Were there's a will; there'll be a family gatherin'.	*Families want to know what will happen to the decrease's possessions.*

Ye'll get yer come-up-ance.	*You will get what is coming to you.*
Between me, you and the gatepost / wall.	*The information is only to be shared between you and another person.*
Ye need to keep yer nose clean.	*You need to stay out of trouble.*
I wouldn't be seen dead at it.	*I don't want to go somewhere.*
There're no back doors in 'im anyway.	*They don't worry about what they say they just come out with it.*
That'll be a whole handlin.	*That is a difficult situation or problem.*
I've the best seat in the house.	*I have a seat at an event which is in a brilliant position and I have a good view.*
Ye can Sally on.	*You can go on by yourself.*
The ball is over the wall.	*It is no longer my responsibility.*
The ball is not in my court now.	*It is up to someone else what they decide to do next.*
It's all a bit of banter anyway.	*It is a bit of fun.*
Ye don't know what yer missin'.	*You don't realise how good it is.*
I don't want to upset the apple cart.	*I do not want to cause trouble.*

Everyone will have to put their shoulder to the wheel.	*Everyone needs to help out.*
The grass doesn't grow under his feet anyway.	*He is always on the move and doesn't stay in one place for long.*
Ye may put a bush in that gap.	*Get a draft excluder.*
You're only as good as yer last match or yer last time out.	*People will only rate you on how well you performed in your last game.*
He's tearin' the arse out of it now.	*He is saying or doing something after everyone else is finished.*
Ye haven't lived.	*You're missing something brilliant.*

I don't want to upset the apple kart

The pot callin' the kettle black.	*You are as equally guilty as someone else.*
It's easy to halve the potato where there love is.	*It is easier to share with the people you love.*
The shit has hit the fan.	*A situation has rapidly deteriorated or has suddenly gone wrong.*
Ye cannot beat experience.	*It is hard to beat someone who has previous knowledge of something.*
I'll get ye in the long grass.	*I will have my revenge.*
We were doin' ok 'til they started to turn the screw on us.	*We were fine until the pressure was increased.*
Ye fell on yer feet / you're landed / that's ye made for life.	*You were very lucky or successful.*
That's light out of an ole moon.	*Someone who you have not heard from in a long time suddenly appears.*
What goes on holidays stays on holidays.	*Keep holiday events a secret.*
It's six of the one an' half a dozen of the other.	*It is the same thing.*
He'll be alright if nothin' falls on him an' it's not too heavy.	*He will be alright if nothing goes wrong.*

Ye may count yer blessings / yer lucky stars.	*Be grateful for what you have.*
That sarcasm doesn't suit ye.	*A person who is sarcastic to you and it is out of character for them to be so.*
Stop pullin' my leg / why don't ye pull my other leg there while you're at it.	*Stop trying to fool me.*
They're both tied to the one stick.	*The same thing is going to happen to two different people.*
It has gone to pot.	*It has been ruined.*
He's really startin' to push the boat out now.	*He is beginning to annoy me / he is being extravagant.*
Yer head must be cut if you're gonna do that!	*You must be crazy to attempt something that is idiotic.*
I'd rather him than me.	*I am glad that is not happening to me.*
I got wind of that happenin'.	*I heard that was going to happen.*
Ye always have to start somewhere.	*You have to start at the beginning.*
I know that road like the back of my hand.	*I have a detailed knowledge of the area.*
That would be a sight for sore eyes.	*It would be good to see that.*

A lesser job would do ye.	*You are not good at what you are attempting.*
I love to hear frogs fartin' in long grass.	*It will have no impact.*
I've that many of them, I could start sellin' them.	*I possess a lot of similar items.*
You're quare an' sure of yourself.	*You are very confident.*
I've been run off my feet lately / rushed off my feet.	*I have been very busy in recent weeks.*
You'd beat the child for doin' that.	*If a child did that it would have been punished.*
Say nothin' or he'll flip the lip.	*Don't say anything because he will get angry.*
The longest road out is the shortest road home.	*Don't attempt short cuts.*
Ye should strike when the iron is hot / the goin' is good.	*You should do it before the opportunity is lost.*
There's no point in makin' a song an' dance outa it.	*Complaining about something won't make a difference.*
Ye learn somethin' new every day.	*You learn new information that surprises you.*
Tailor made to fit.	*Something that fits exactly in a certain place as if it was specially made to fit there.*

That was a bit of a close shave / I wouldn't like to be as close to death.	*That was a narrow escape.*
They must have got the wrong end of the stick.	*They must have misunderstand what was said.*
He's goin' the wrong road.	*His future is uncertain or his life could end badly.*
It's not worth the hassle.	*It is more trouble than it is worth.*
They're very easy to wind up.	*They are easily annoyed.*
I'll torture them like a bad smell.	*I will keep annoying them.*
I'm goin' to bury the hatchet with them.	*I am going to stop fighting with them.*
Give a man enough rope an' he'll hang himself.	*If you want someone's true character to be revealed, let them keep talking.*
They're only a pen pusher.	*They are office workers.*
Whatever he doesn't know isn't worth knowin'.	*He is very knowledgeable.*
I don't even have the time to bless myself.	*I am extremely busy and I have no time to anything.*
Ye might as well be ravin' in bed as revin' there.	*Nobody's listening to what you are saying.*
They do a lot of bummin' an' blowin'.	*They boost a lot.*

You've earned yer corn today anyway.

You have worked hard for your wages.

Don't throw out yer dirty water 'til you've the clean water in.

Don't throw something out until you have a replacement.

It was full to the rafters / it was bunged.

There was a large crowd.

There's one far ye!

That will surprise you.

More power til' yer elbow.

Good luck to you.

I wouldn't give him the skin off ma skitter!

You wouldn't give him anything.

That's a load of balls.

That's rubbish.

Get tore into them lads!

To do something with enthusiasm.

I wouldn't hear tell of it.

I don't believe it.

Don't shite on yer own doorstep.

Don't do anything which might end affecting you in the future.

Ye could take them nowhere.

They mess around or cause havoc everywhere they go.

I'm glad to see the back of ye / it.

I am pleased that something is finished.

Ye'd think that they owned the place.

They think they are above everyone else.

He'd turn in his grave if he knew that.	*That would have really annoyed the decreased.*
More Irish graves are opened by the mouth than the spade.	*Irish people usually end up saying the wrong things and end up in trouble.*
I'm not goin' to get mixed up in that.	*I am not getting involved.*
It must be as old as Methuselah.	*It is extremely old.*
I got enough or seen enough to do ma.	*I am satisfied and do not want to see anymore.*
Don't pay any heed on him.	*Don't pay any attention.*
Talkin' when he should have been listenin'.	*He should have listened.*
I was beside myself.	*I was very upset about something.*
If ye walk with lame people ye'll soon walk with a limp yourself.	*Unsavoury people can have a bad influence on you.*
She's never off the bat.	*She is always busy.*
He's out on his own now.	*He is self-employed.*
Ye wouldn't make it in time unless ye had an aerolane.	*It seems impossible to reach the destination within that time.*
May the road rise up before.	*May you be successful in the future.*

Chapter 6

Insults & Appearance

Yer head is so big that ye'll never get through that door!

They always make a meal of everythin' / make a mountain out of a molehill.	*They make a big issue out of a minor problem.*
Ye always seem to put a dampner on things.	*You make things less enjoyable.*
His / her head is stuck in the clouds.	*He /she does not have any sense.*
Ye wouldn't know a good horse if it hit ye in the face.	*You do not understand the concept of picking a good competitor.*
They're always harpin' on about somethin'.	*They are always complaining.*
They love themselves that much that they'd marry themselves if they could.	*They have very high opinions of themselves.*
Somethin' must have crawled up inside ye and died.	*You have just farted and it smells really bad.*
I want the news not the weather.	*I don't want to be spat on.*
Say it don't spray it.	*I would rather you didn't spit on me whilst you are talking.*
You're just a thorn in my side.	*You are a nuisance.*
Ye may open that window an' let yer head out or ye'll never get through that door because yer head is so big.	*You are conceited.*

They're like a bad rash they wouldn't leave ye alone.	*They are a nuisance.*
Yer writin' is like double Dutch to me.	*Your writing is very hard to read.*
Look at the shot of him / the hack of him.	*Someone who looks to have let their personal appearance or hygiene go.*
Ye can grow up anytime.	*You are childish.*
They haven't got a note in their head.	*An individual who cannot sing.*
She was plastered in make-up / caked / baked in it.	*To have a large amount of make-up on your face in an effort to look more attractive.*
Ye could pinch an inch or two on ye!	*Said to an overweight person who has excess fat and can be easily pinched.*
He thought he was smart but his plan back fired on him.	*A person had a clever idea but it didn't work out for them and it all went wrong.*
Get the violins out for him.	*Expect a sob story.*
You're that acute / awkward that ye couldn't even lie in bed straight.	*An awkward person who always does things their own way.*
I wouldn't spit on ye if ye were on fire.	*I don't like you at all.*
Were ye drunk when ye put that wallpaper on?	*Wallpaper which has not been hung on the wall straight.*

The wallpaper in yer house is up an' down like the waves of Torri.	*Anything which isn't straight or even.*
Ye couldn't hit water if ye fell out of a boat.	*A person who has a bad aim when they are trying to hit a target.*
Quit yer gurnin'.	*Stop complaining.*
They'd soon tell ye a big one / tell ye a lie that would hang ye.	*They would tell you a huge story which is totally untrue.*
You're as ole as tea.	*You are old.*
They're clean done / they're over the hill.	*A person who is no longer capable.*
I see you're flyin' yer trousers at half mask today.	*Your trousers are above your waist line.*
Ye'd think that they had a poker stuck up their arse.	*Walking with a very straight back.*
Were ye brought up or dragged up?	*Those who are badly behaved.*
It'd be cheaper to keep a photograph of ye.	*An extravagant person.*
There're only two gears in him, dead slow and stop.	*People who do everything at a very slow pace.*
You're only an ole crock.	*You appear to have bad health.*
Look at the cut a ye.	*You are very untidy.*

Listenin' to them is like listenin' to a broken record.	*They continually complain.*
With a name like that yer parents mustn't have liked ye.	*A person's name which you are not particularly fond of.*
You're only a turn coat.	*You have decided to support a different political party, team or church.*
They like to hear themselves talkin'.	*They talk too much.*
Ye must be havin' a bad hair day / yer hair is like a crow's nest.	*You have messy or untidy hair.*
I miss ye like a sore head.	*I am glad to get rid of you.*
They should get an Oscar.	*They are good at acting or pretending that there is something wrong with them.*
You're livin' in a dream world.	*You imagine things which you think you could not achieve.*
There's wiser than him chewin' grass, lookin' over the hedge or locked up.	*They are stupid.*
Ye smell like a wet dog in the summertime.	*You smell extremely bad.*
His breath would knock ye out / they've got dog breath.	*He has bad breath.*
I'm goin' to give him a mouth ful'.	*I am going to tell him what I think of him.*

There are more guts in a heron than ye.	*You are a cowardly person.*
They're that stuck up that they wouldn't even look at ye / they'd let on that they didn't see ye.	*They do not take you under their notice because they feel above you.*
I'm laughin' at ye not with ye!	*You are foolish.*
They're only a pair of 'coffin dodgers'.	*They are very old people.*
They're no relation of mine.	*They have nothing to do with me.*
Those trousers you've on are that big that ye could put two people in them.	*Have you lost weight?*
If they smiled their face would crack.	*They rarely ever smile.*
Their breath is that bad that ye could cut it with a knife.	*They have really bad breath.*
Ye couldn't organise a dog fight / a piss up in a brewery.	*You have very poor organisational skills.*
They've their own graveyard with no one in it.	*They make empty threats about beating up people.*
There's four eyes comin' up the street now.	*There's someone who wears glasses.*
Yer eyes must be drawn on or else painted on.	*You have poor eyesight.*

They'd need an exhaust pipe fitted to them.	*They tend to pass wind quite often.*
He's stuck in everythin' but the crib.	*He is involved in many different activities or clubs.*
That's not my child anyway it must have been switched at birth.	*I am disgraced by my child's behaviour.*
Ye couldn't kill a weed.	*A really bad person never seems to die; it is always the good people who die first.*
It's paintin' a bad picture of him.	*It is giving him a bad public image.*
Ye'd be late for yer own funeral.	*You are not a punctual person.*
I wouldn't go outa the house like that.	*I would not appear anywhere wearing such revealing clothing.*
Yer as popular as a fart in a space suit.	*You are not liked.*
There are more brains in a false face or in my arse than you have.	*You are not intelligent.*
Are ye deaf or just hard of hearin'?	*Used when someone they did not hear what you said.*
She made a haymas of it or ballsed it up.	*She made a mess of it.*

You would need an exhaust pipe fitted.

Ye daren't look at them sideways.	*They are short tempered.*
Look what the cat has dragged in.	*Said to someone who arrives late to a function looking like a mess or flustered.*
You're gona make a pig's ear of it.	*You will make a mess of it.*
They'd start a row in an empty house.	*They are argumentative.*
Yer only a big ginny / big girl's blouse.	*Said to a person who is afraid of doing something.*
They'd fight with their shadows.	*They like to start fights.*

Ye must have no blood in ye.	*You are cold even on a warm day.*
Crooked as a dog's hind leg.	*People who do things to annoy you.*
I wouldn't call the dog that.	*A horrible name for a person.*
They'd argue that a black crow was white.	*They always think they are right even when they are wrong.*
That person must have a chip on their shoulder.	*A person that is unhappy or angry due to past experiences.*
It's nothin' to write home about anyway.	*It was not as good as expected.*
You're yer own worst enemy.	*You are the cause of your own problems.*
They just can't hack it.	*You can not cope with a task you were given.*
There's always one.	*There is always someone who causes trouble.*
If they can do it anyone can.	*People who you believe are less capable than you can do something then anyone can.*
All nice to yer face, but they'd stab ye in the back.	*They are hypocrites.*
They're showin' their true colours now.	*Their true nature is apparent now.*

They're a breed of their own.	*They are different from the rest of us.*
Yer house is like a 'duckle'.	*Your house is filthy.*
The daughter is no angel but the father could be the devil.	*The father's even worse than the daughter.*
They're a lose canon.	*They are foolish and unpredictable.*
Ye couldn't hold yer piss.	*You can't keep a secret.*
You've a tongue on ye that would clip hedges.	*You use foul or inappropriate language in the present of others.*
A bad penny always turns up.	*Rascals always arrive.*
Ye couldn't put a patch on 'em.	*You are not as talented as they are.*
Too sweet to be wholesome.	*Someone who you believe are far too nice and that they are not actually genuine.*
They'd tell ye their life story.	*They tell you irrelevant information about themselves.*
Ye could drive a wheel barrow / bus through their legs.	*Bow legged people.*
Some people couldn't put a patch on yer arse.	*Those people that can not mend anything.*
If he does that I'll eat my cap.	*I will be surprised if he succeeds.*

They have let the side down.	*They have disappointed a number of people.*

How to insult someone's partner...

She's no spring chicken anyway.	*She is not young.*
He's just a big blow watch he doesn't blow ye away.	*He boosts a lot about what he owns or what he has done.*
She's that ugly that the tide wouldn't take 'er out.	*She is so ugly that no one would date her.*
He'd give ye the skitter!	*He would annoy you and get on your nerves.*
They couldn't sing for their supper.	*Those people that can not sing.*

Ye could drive a wheelbarrow through your legs

Tryin' to make conversion with them is like pullin' teeth.	*They are difficult to talk to.*
Ye couldn't like him if ye reared him.	*He is a nasty person.*
He's over the top.	*He takes things too far.*
Take everythin' he says with a pinch of salt.	*Don't take anything he tells you seriously as it is more than likely untrue.*
That man has the personality of a brick.	*He has absolutely no personality.*
Their head is up their arse.	*Those who think that you are brilliant but others would not agree.*
He thinks that he's God's gift / the best thing since sliced bread / dog's bollicks.	*He believes he is better than everyone else.*
She's no oil paintin' anyway.	*She is an ugly person.*
If she was a chocolate bar she'd eat herself.	*She loves her own appearance.*
There isn't a manner in him.	*He is bad mannered.*
She's nice from afar but she's far from nice.	*She is attractive looking but has a nasty personality.*
They're wet behind the ears.	*They are immature.*
He stands out like a sore thumb.	*He doesn't fit in.*

She's not up to much.	*She is not attractive.*
That fella is only a mouth.	*He is a very talkative person or he tells lies.*
Ye need to get shot of him.	*You need to get rid of him.*
His shirt would stand itself.	*He smells bad due to body odour.*
They'd talk the hind legs off a donkey.	*They talk excessively and not know when to stop.*
Ye'd think that she had never farted before.	*Everyone passes wind it's natural but there are those who are so posh that you would think they never* DID *it.*
He'd argue with his fingernail.	*An argumentative person.*
She's like mutton dressed as lamb.	*A mature woman dressed in a like a younger lady.*
That man is as odd as a nine pound note / he's as odd as seven.	*He is an introverted person who doesn't like to socialise.*

Insults aimed at men

He smells like a jack donkey.	*He smells bad due to excessive sweating.*
He's lost his marbles.	*He has bad nerves.*
He'd go to the openin' of a letter.	*He would attend anything.*

You'd hear him long before you'd see him.	*He is a loud or boisterous person.*
He smells that bad that even the pigs would put 'im out.	*He has an extremely bad body odour.*
He hangs his fiddle on the door.	*He acts differently when he is at home than he does when he is in public.*
They can talk the talk but can they walk the walk?	*They boast about what they will do, but it is not known if they're capable of anything.*
He never brings anythin' new to the table.	*He has no new ideas.*
His work is amateur.	*His work isn't any good.*
He's just a picture an' no sound.	*He doesn't say anything.*
He couldn't read the truth outa the bible.	*He is a compulsive liar.*
He doesn't have many bars in his gate. ? GRATE?	*He has lost a lot of his teeth.*
He always tells me a joke with a jag.	*He is sarcastic.*
He would start a fight with his own shadow.	*He is very argumentative.*
He's rotten to the core.	*He is an evil person.*
He has a bit of a head about himself.	*He thinks he is better than everyone else.*

He smells that bad, ye could hunt 'im.	*He is so smelly hounds could find him easily.*
He's just not cut out for it.	*He is not well suited or qualified for it.*
That fella is always actin' the buck eejit.	*He is always acting stupid.*
He'd take ye 'round the country for a shortcut / near cut.	*He will take a longer route believing it's a short cut.*
If he was shot he'd never fall.	*He has huge feet.*
He runs everyone into the ground.	*He speaks ill of everyone.*
He couldn't spell his own name.	*He can't spell.*
He's like an ole man of the mountains.	*He appears to be a lot older than he is.*
He's on the road to no town.	*He is going nowhere.*
Yer man is fly but I never seen 'im shite on the ceilin'.	*He is a sly or cunning person.*
He has two left feet.	*He is clumsy.*
He'd run all night an' lie all day.	*He stays out all night and sleep all day.*
He lives in them clothes.	*He wears the same clothes all the time.*

Don't ask him for anythin' because ye'll be there all night.	*He is a very talkative person and engages in deep conversations.*
He hasn't a great word to say about anyone.	*He is critical of everyone.*
He couldn't crack an egg, there's no power in him at all.	*He has little or no strength.*
My ears are sore listenin' to him all day.	*He talks too much.*
He's just like a chocolate man.	*He is someone who always seems to have an injury.*
The only time ye see him is when he's lookin' somethin'.	*You only ever see him when he needs something off you.*
Ye could get yer breakfast outa his hair.	*Bits of food stuck in his hair.*
He couldn't run the length of himself.	*He is unfit.*
He'd bet on two flies goin' up the wall.	*He would gamble his money on anything.*

Insults aimed at women

She's been just sittin' there like a clockin' hen.	*She has been sitting in the same place for a long period of time.*
She knows how to milk it.	*She knows how to benefit herself as much as possible.*

If ye hit 'er you'd break 'er like an egg.	*She is thin or a really weak person.*
She has a fair bit of mileage up.	*She is quite old.*
She has that much grease in 'er hair that ye could oil a chip pan with it.	*She has very greasy hair.*
That woman is as deaf as a post.	*She has poor hearing.*
She mustn't get out much.	*She hasn't seen a lot.*
Ye couldn't get a word in with 'er edgeways.	*She talks too much and never gives you a chance to speak.*
She's as wicked as a weasel.	*She is a cross individual and can be nasty towards others.*
If ye can't lift 'er don't shift 'er.	*Don't date a fat woman.*
She's like a lap dog / she's like ringworm / a bad rash.	*She will follow you around a lot and is hard to get rid of.*

Describin' someone's face

That man's face looks like a burnt out fuse box.	*He has got an ugly face.*
You've a face on ye like a hatchet.	*You have a very sharp or pointed face.*
She's a face on 'er like a wet week.	*She has a really sour look on her face.*

You've a face on ye like a busted boot.

You have a face that is not pleasing to the eye.

She has a face on her like a bulldog chewin' a wasp.

Her face is always screwed up.

He's a face like a shovel.

He has a very square and flat face.

They had a face on them that would stop a watch.

They have an extremely unpleasant looking face.

She has a face on 'er like a smacked arse.

She has a really bright red face / rosy cheeks.

He must have caught their face in a door.

He has an ugly or bad looking face.

Your face looks like my arse!

He has a face like a well chewed wriggly.	*His face is like a piece of chewing gum.*
If I hit ye a slap on the back yer face would fall off.	*You wear a lot of makeup.*
Yer face looks like my arse.	*You are ugly.*
A face that would turn milk.	*An unpleasant looking face.*

Stupid people

They haven't a brain cell among them.	*They are stupid.*
If brains were dynamite, ye wouldn't have enough to blow yer own nose.	*You have little or no intelligence.*
That lad needs his head looked.	*He doesn't know what he is doing.*
Ye haven't an ounce of sense.	*You have absolutely no sense and does very stupid things.*
They'd know more about a fish supper.	*They know very little but think they know everything.*
I think that they're only about half in it.	*They lack understanding.*
Ye could write what he knows on the back of a stamp.	*He has a poor knowledge or understanding of a particular subject.*
They're as thick as a ditch.	*They are not smart.*

They haven't got the brains they were born with.	*They are not intelligent.*
I forgot more than ye'll ever know.	*You are uneducated.*
He has as much clue about that as the man on the moon.	*He has absolutely no idea about what he is doing.*
They aren't the full shillin'.	*They do not behave in an appropriate manner and tends to do silly things.*
They don't know their arse from their elbow / hole in the ground.	*Someone who can't tell the difference in two things which are completely different.*

Crazy people

They must be losin' the plot.	*They are doing things which are out of character.*
You've a wee want in ye.	*You act stupidly or inappropriately for their age.*
They must be away in the head.	*They are not acting logically.*
His head is full of wee doors an' they're all bangin'.	*He is crazy.*
I think they must have a few slates missin' on the roof / the light is on but there's no one in / at home.	*They do things which are totally stupid and there is no logic in what they do.*

That person is a head the ball.	*A crazy person.*
You're not all there.	*You are not mentally competent.*
They're a sandwich short of picnic.	*They do not act in a sensible manner.*
I don't think he's playin' with a full deck.	*He is stupid.*
They're wired up but not plugged in.	*They always say or do silly things.*
I don't believe the lift goes all the way to the top.	*Those people who don't consider intelligent.*
You're like the fool Lavery's.	*You are acting foolishly.*
He wouldn't know if a dog bit him.	*He has little or no sense.*
They must be away with the fairies.	*They talk about things which don't make any sense.*
The wheel is goin' round but the hamster is gone.	*A person who seems ok but act stupid.*

Useless people

He's that useless that he'd bend a crowbar in a bog.	*He is a poor workman.*
My back is sore holdin' the rest of the team up.	*I am tired of doing more than my fair share.*

You're full of big ideas an' nothin' at the arse of it.	*You have huge ambitions but you end up doing very little.*
Ye couldn't box eggs.	*You're not a good fighter.*
They're a dead loss.	*They are incapable of doing anything.*
He couldn't hit a bull in the arse with a bakin' board.	*He has a very poor shot or sense of direction.*
Ye couldn't drive a nail in a turnip.	*You have no strength.*
They're a complete waste of space.	*They are utterly useless.*
Them ones couldn't rear a dog.	*They couldn't look after an animal properly never mind a human being.*
Ye do everythin' arse about face.	*You do everything the wrong way round.*
He wouldn't know to take his feet outa his dinner.	*He has no sense.*
Ye couldn't kill a fly / bust a paper bag / give a hen the heartburn.	*You have little or no strength.*
He couldn't clean his own face never mind anythin' else.	*He is not good at cleaning anything including his own body.*
You're as useless as a chocolate fireguard.	*You are incapable of completing a task they were given.*

If I were you, I'd hang up the boots.	*You should just give up.*
Ye couldn't find Holy Water in a chapel.	*You are very bad at finding things even if they are located near you.*
He hasn't hands on him to bless himself.	*He is incapable of doing anything.*
I wouldn't see ye in my road.	*To state that you work a lot harder than someone else.*
Ye'd forget yer head if it wasn't attached to yer body.	*You are a very forgetful person.*
All you're good for is trampin' grass.	*You are not good at playing field games.*
Ye could beat him with yer cap.	*He could be easily defeated.*
They couldn't win an argument.	*They rarely win anything.*
He couldn't beat his way out of a wet paper bag.	*He is absolutely no good at fighting.*
If there were two eggs in a bowl ye'd struggle to beat them.	*You who could not beat anyone in a fight.*
He couldn't score furniture / he couldn't score in a brothel.	*He would find it hard to score during a game.*
Ye couldn't stop an alarm clock / the bread man.	*Said to a goalkeeper to highlight how bad you think they are.*

He couldn't shoot marbles	*He has a very bad aim.*
Ye couldn't beat eggs with an electric whisk.	*You are really bad at fighting.*
He couldn't catch the cold.	*He is not good at catching a ball.*
As useless as the left side of the countdown clock.	*Countdown is a popular TV program and one side of the clock does nothing.*
As useful as a white crayon.	*Someone who is no good at doing anything and is rarely ever asked to do much.*
As useless as a sore thumb.	*A person who you think is not capable of doing anything right.*
As useless as a lighthouse in a bog / tits on a bull.	*You don't posses much skill.*
As useless as a hand brake on a canoe.	*No use or pointless.*

Skinny people

You're built like a greyhound.	*You have a slim and muscular frame.*
He must have the hind teat.	*He is very thin.*
There are more muscles on my finger than ye have.	*You have little or no muscle on your body.*
She hasn't a pick on 'er.	*She is very thin.*

He's a bit gawky lookin'.	*He is skinny.*
They've failed away to nothin'.	*They lost a lot of weight.*
You're that thin that ye could fall down a gratin.	*You are very thin.*
There's more meat on a butcher's pencil.	*A person or animal that is very thin and has no flesh on them.*
He / she is built like a tooth pick.	*A tall, skinny person.*
I've seen more muscles in a bag of winkles.	*To have a poor physic and no muscle on your body.*
He could kiss a goat between the horns.	*He has a thin face.*
If ye looked at them from the side, ye wouldn't see them at all.	*They are extremely thin with small waistlines.*
His legs are like two pins or sticks.	*He has two very thin legs.*
As thin as a rake / they're like a bean pole.	*A skinny person who has not got much fat.*

Tall people

If ye were any longer ye'd be late.	*A really tall individual.*

If he fell twice he'd be home.	*He is a very tall person*
Ye must have been grown out of a flowerpot.	*He is a really tall person.*

Fat people

He's the size of a house.	*He is overweight.*
As wide as a ditch.	*Over-weight.*
You've fairly put on the beef lately.	*You have recently gained a lot of weight.*
They've an arse on them like the back end of a bus.	*They have a wide or fat backside.*
I don't know how she got into that dress, she must have been launched into it an' she'll have to be cut out of it.	*You do not understand how someone physically got into a dress or how she will get out of it again.*
The buttons are bustin' open on his shirt like my granny's busted slipper.	*He is so fat that they busting out of their shirt.*
He has more chins than a Chinese phonebook.	*He has a double chin.*
Ye'd think that someone put a foot pump to ye.	*You have got fat.*
That would be a big cage to clean out.	*A fat person would excrete more than a smaller person.*
As fat as a fool.	*A very overweight or obese person.*

He / she has more rolls than a bakery.	*Someone who has many rolls of fat.*
They're startin' to fairly pile on the pounds.	*They have gained a lot of weight recently.*

Ugly people

They'd need rubbed out an' drew over again.	*They are so ugly that they would need to be completely changed.*
Yer teeth are like a row of bombed houses.	*A person who is missing quite a number of front teeth.*
He's like somethin' that fell off a tinker's cart an' wasn't missed.	*A mean looking person.*
Her hair is like rat's tails.	*Untidy hair.*
They could eat an apple though a tennis racquet.	*Someone who has prominent front teeth.*
She looks alright 'til ye sober up.	*You think someone looks lovely when you're drunk but not when you are sober.*
They weren't blessed with good looks anyway.	*A person who you find unattractive.*

Chapter 7
Threats

I will hang ye out to dry!

Don't breathe a word of it to anyone / don't tell a sinner.	*Keep something a secret.*
Ye could find yourself in deep water very quickly.	*You could get yourself into trouble.*
He has to be shown who's boss.	*To show someone that you have power and authority over them.*
Ye need to start pullin' yer weight.	*You should do your bit.*
He'll be the one who ends up with egg on his face.	*He will be the one who will end up being humiliated.*
You're barkin' up the wrong tree.	*You picked the wrong person or idea.*
Someday he'll meet his match.	*He will eventually meet someone who is equally as good as him and he won't be able to beat them.*
They've over stepped the mark or they've crossed the line.	*They have taken things too far and now they will have to suffer the consequences.*
Ye need to stand up and be counted.	*You must your opinions known even if it may get you into trouble.*
Mind yer own business and let others mind theirs.	*Don't get involved in other people's problems or personal issues.*
Ye have te toe the line.	*You have to do as you are told.*

Ye could end up in a heap of bother.	*You could get yourself into a lot of trouble with other people or the authorities.*
Don't be givin' me any of yer ole buck.	*Don't be cheeky.*
Wind yer neck in!	*Don't be so cheeky / cocky.*

Physical threats

Watch yer face, in case I shove it through the back of yer neck.	*To inform someone of how hard you are going to hit them.*
Yer face will look like a welder's glove when I've finished with ye.	*Your face will look very badly torn after I have beaten you up.*
You've got off lightly so far but ye could be in for it yet.	*You have been lucky but it could still land you in trouble.*
The bigger ye are, the harder ye fall.	*Said to a large person that you intend to beat regardless of their height.*
You're cruisin' for a bruisin'.	*If you carry on behaving or talking the way you are, you will be hit by the person you are upsetting.*
Ye need yer wings clipped and I'm the man to do it.	*You are acting too clever. It can also mean to reduce or put an end to someone's privileges.*

Yer boot should never be outa his arse, only when you're swingin' it.

He needs to be constantly kicked on the arse.

He'll only do that the once.

If he does that there will be severe consequences and he won't be able to do it again as he will be so badly beaten.

Ye'll be lickin' yer wounds tomorrow.

To spend time getting yourself back to full strength after getting badly hurt.

Do that again an' ye'll be a week dead next Saturday.

To make a threat to kill someone today, making them a week dead next week.

Many a time a man's mouth broke his nose.

You need to be careful what you say because you could end up getting beaten.

Do ye want a dig in the bake?

Would you like me to punch you in the face?

Stop cryin' or I'll give somethin' to cry about.

Usually said to someone who is crying over something silly. You threaten them by saying that if they don't stop crying you will hurt them.

If yer lookin' a kickin' you're goin' the right road about it.

You are starting to get on someone's nerves.

I'm gona batter yer mate.

I am going to hit your friend.

Ah'll knack yer ballax in!

I will beat you senseless.

Shut yer gub or I'll shut it for ye!	*Stop talking or I will leave you unable to talk!*
I bate bigger men to get into a row.	*I am not one bit afraid of you.*
Do ye want a belly full of teeth an' a mouth full of knuckles?	*Do you want all your teeth knocked out?*
I'll do yer knees in.	*I will injure your knees.*
I'll knack two layers of shite outa ye!	*I am going to badly beat you.*
I'll do ye in.	*I am going to kill you.*
I'll beat him like a bad dog.	*I will beat you easily.*
I'll hit ye a clout in the lug.	*I will hit you.*
I'll re-arrange yer face for ye, if ye don't be careful.	*I intend to hit you with such force that your face will be disfigured.*
I'll soon show him who is boss.	*I will make it clear to him that I have more power or authority than they do.*
I'll come off ya as quick as I would look at ye.	*I will hit you just as fast as I could look at you.*
I'll leave ye drinkin' through a straw.	*I will knock your teeth out.*
I'll have his guts for garter.	*I am going to punish him very severely.*

I'll knock ye into the middle of next week.	*The expression is used to emphasise how hard you intend to hit someone.*
I'll knock yer pan in.	*I intend to hit you on the head.*
I'll hang ye out to dry.	*I will leave you in a bad state or abandon you when you are in trouble.*
I'll rip yer head off an' shite on yer neck.	*A statement of an intention to inflict a lot of pain on a person who you have no respect for them.*
I'll beat the linin' / stuffin' / daylights outa ye.	*I am going to beat you so much that your internal organs will come out.*
I'll bate ye good lookin'.	*You will beat someone up.*
I'll give ye the Lord's prayer.	*Threatening to hit someone.*
I'll malou / bury ye.	*I will beat you up.*
I'll clean yer clock / clean ye out.	*I will beat you up.*

Psychological threats

Yer days are numbered.	*You haven't long left.*
You've beaten all the rest so now ye have to beat the best.	*A phrase said when you have beaten many different people, but your next opponent is the champion.*

Don't worry; I'll wipe the smile off yer face.	*To do something on someone which will make them less confident.*
I'll take ye to the cleaners.	*I will take your assets. It can also mean to beat someone by a great margin at a sport.*
Yer card has been marked.	*You have been identified as a target.*
It's about time ye stood on yer own two feet.	*You need to be independent.*
Ye don't want to rub me up the wrong road / way.	*It would be unwise to annoy or irritate me as it you could end up getting hurt.*
Don't start somethin' that ye can't finish.	*There is no point starting a fight if you can't finish it.*
Yer gettin' too big for yer boots.	*You behave as if you are more important or clever than you actually are.*
It's about time ye woke up an' smelt the roses.	*You need to catch on to what you should be doing with your life.*
I'll make him eat his words.	*I will make him admit he was wrong to boost or threaten another person.*
A little dog can start a hare, but it takes a big dog to finish it.	*A small person can often start a fight but it takes a bigger person to finish it.*

Don't let yer tongue cut yer throat.	*Don't say anything which could upset someone because you could end up getting hurt or even killed over it.*
We'll see how good ye are when the tables are turned.	*It will be interesting to see how you cope when things are the opposite of what they used to be.*
All talk and no action.	*Someone who boasts a lot and promises many things but does very little.*
You're on a very slippery slope.	*Things are going to start going wrong for you in the future.*
I'll tie ye up in knots.	*I will make it hard for you to do anything.*
I'll beat ye by a country mile.	*I will beat you by a clear margin or a great distance.*
I'll beat ye at yer own game / I'll give ye a taste of yer own medicine.	*To get something done on you which you have done to everyone else.*
I'll take ye out by the root.	*I will beat you by a clear margin or to hit someone hard.*
Ye may pull yer horns in.	*You must restrain someone's ardour or lower your ambitions. It can also mean to spend less money.*
It's only lent to ye.	*You will get revenge on someone in the future.*

Don't show yer teeth 'til ye can bite.	*Don't make threats that you are not capable of carrying out.*
'Tis a long road that there's no turn on.	*You will get someone back in the future for doing something on you.*
Long run the fox.	*Eventually someone will get their comeuppance i.e. justice will be served on them through time.*
Don't mess with the best because the best don't mess.	*You have no chance of winning.*
You're only diggin' a bigger hole for yourself.	*You need to stop talking because you are only getting yourself into more trouble.*
I'll teach ye a thing or two.	*I know many ways in which I can get what I want.*
Ye should clean up 'round yer own door before ye say anythin' about anyone else's!	*Don't criticize anyone else you should mind your own business.*
The only time I was beat was when I wasn't there.	*I have never been beaten.*
Don't start ma.	*To imply that if you get annoyed then someone will end up getting hurt.*

Chapter 8
'Norn Iron'

That will be brushed under the carpet

I don't know whether I'm comin' or goin'.	*I am so busy that I don't know what I am doing.*
Could ye run yer eye over that?	*Tell me what you think of that.*
He's only tryin' to stitch ye up.	*He is trying to humilliate you.*
I'd see ye in hell before I'd do that.	*I will not do that.*
That would be right up yer street.	*Anything that you like to do and that you enjoy doing.*
It wouldn't be my cup of tea anyway.	*Refers to something that you wouldn't like.*
I'm that low I can't even put my hand up to touch the bottom.	*I feel very depressed or ill.*
There's enough of eejits goin' without me goin' too.	*I do not want to go.*
He keeps himself to himself.	*He doesn't get involved with others.*
I could see him far enough.	*I do not like him.*
That'll suit ye down till the ground.	*Something which you really like doing.*
I'll get the brownie points up for that.	*I will get credit for doing that.*
They've been there a lifetime.	*They have been in the same place or job for a long time.*

I think I'll put it on the long finger.	*I will put off doing that for a while.*
I'd advise ye to keep them at arm's length.	*A person who you would prefer not to be around.*
I was in stitches / killin' myself / I nearly wet myself / splittin' my sides laughin'.	*I was laughing uncontrollably at something.*
Watch what ye say when you're 'round them because their ears will be flappin'.	*Nosey people who are filled with curiosity.*
Ye may just hold fire.	*Be patient and wait to see how other things go first.*
They're all on the brew.	*They are unemployed people receiving benefits from the government.*
I was eggin' him on to do it.	*I encouraged him to do that.*
I'm sick, sore an' tired of tellin' ye that.	*I am fed up telling you the same information.*
I might be able to pull a few strings.	*I might be able to help you.*
Ye'd need to be up an' be on the ball.	*You need to be alert and ready to go.*
Who does he think he is?	*A cheeky or arrogant person.*
Any word of ye?	*Are you up out of bed yet?*
Quit yer talkin'!	*You find it hard to believe what someone is telling you.*

Now yer talkin'!	*You like what someone has just told you.*
Are ye gettin' 'er handy?	*Are you finding that easy?*
Who's he, when he's right an' home?	*You are wondering who someone is.*
That's it out the window now.	*That's finished it with.*
My head has been splittin' all day.	*I have a really sore head.*
We're all just sittin' about lookin' at each other.	*We weren't doing anything.*
I'll tell ye on the QT.	*Keep this a secret.*
I'll tell this but it is off the cuff.	*Sharing information which you are not meant to.*
Ye'll know yer maker when that happens.	*That will be a major test.*
That's all dead an' buried.	*It's all over or finished with so you can forget about it.*
Keep an eye out for them?	*To watch for someone arriving.*
They think they know everythin' about everybody.	*They will to know or discuss everyone's business.*
Ye'd need to be thick skinned 'round 'ere.	*You don't need to be sensitive or take offence easily.*
They can give plenty of it but they can't take it.	*They enjoy making fun of others but hate it done them.*

I did it 'til I was blue in the face.	*Continually doing something over and over again.*
That'll drive me 'round the bend.	*I am getting frustrated.*
They're gona drive me up the walls.	*They are getting on my nerves.*
I'm not just doin' it for the good of ma health.	*I am doing something which needs to be done or which I am being paid for.*
I could write a book about him / her.	*Refers to someone who you know a lot about.*
They've some neck on 'em to do that / they've a brass neck.	*They would do anything or say anything to anyone.*
I need that like a hole in the head.	*Something that I don't require.*
They'll not know what hit them.	*They have taken on a task but do not realise how hard it will actually be.*
They open their mouth an' words come out.	*They do not think before they speak.*
He has had that for forever and a day.	*He has had that for a long time.*
I never heard the like of it.	*That is astonishing.*
He's just gettin' back on his feet again.	*He's recovering from an illness or it can mean a business is recovering.*

I haven't got a baldy.	*I don't have a clue what you are talking about.*
There's no call to eat the head off me.	*There is no reason for you to be annoyed with me.*
You're not takin' much hurt anyway.	*You are lucky that you have nothing to do.*
They nearly jumped outa their skin.	*They were frightened or shocked.*
You've two hopes, Bob hope an' no hope.	*There is no hope of something happening.*
Ye know the score anyway.	*You are well informed.*
They're very dry on it.	*They don't say much to you or someone who you find difficult to make conversion with.*
We're not outa the woods yet.	*We are not out of trouble yet.*
I'm signin' my life away.	*I have to sign my name many times on a document and I'm unsure what it is for.*
He's a holy Joe.	*He is good living.*
They're always huggin' the altar rails.	*They attend Church regularly.*
The house was a kip.	*The house was very untidy or filthy.*
It was a piece of cake or it was wee buns.	*A task which was easy to complete.*

Ye wouldn't see him from one weekend to the next.	*You rarely ever see him.*
I can see a different side to them now.	*I have a better understanding of them now.*
They'll probably turn a blind eye til' it.	*They will pretend they didn't see it.*
Same shit, different day.	*Same situation, different time.*
We're both in the same boat.	*We are both in the same situation.*
They were scared outa their wits.	*They were extremely frightened.*
Ye just got me on the hop.	*I wasn't expecting you.*
How are ya keepin'?	*How are you?*
Ah, I'm strugglin' on!	*I'm fine.*
What goes 'round comes 'round.	*Actions have consequences.*
There's no holdin' him back.	*He is getting on well.*
It takes one to know one.	*A person is expressing criticism but they have similar faults to the person being criticized.*
That's half the battle.	*That's the most difficult part of a process but, once you have it completed, you have almost succeeded.*

Stall the ball a minute.	*Hold on a minute, don't do anything immediately.*
You've had too many birthdays.	*You are getting old.*
They're only beatin' the water with a stick.	*It won't make any difference.*
Well, it's neither here nor there.	*It doesn't matter.*
Stop actin' like Jack the lad.	*Don't be acting like a fool.*
Couldn't make head nor tail of it.	*You couldn't understand something.*
The tears were trippin' him.	*He was crying uncontrollably.*
I'm gona get offside.	*I am having nothing to do with it.*
It's all much of a muchness.	*It's all same.*
Ye must have put the skud on ma.	*You wished bad luck on me.*
They were up from the crack of dawn.	*They were up early.*
He'll be there 'til the death anyway.	*He will stay a long time.*
It's just one thing after another.	*One problem happens and then another one occurs.*
I've got the jist of it now.	*I understand what's going on.*

You're only a number at the end of the day.	*You don't seem to matter in a large company or group of people.*
Don't let them walk all over ye, stand yer ground with them.	*You need to be more assertive.*
Oh that's over my head; I wouldn't know anythin' about that!	*It's something that is too complicated for me.*
They can do no wrong.	*They always seem to get everything right and never make any mistakes.*
I'll just have te bite my lip.	*I am extremely annoyed but I don't want to say anything.*
We'll just have te wait 'til it takes its toll.	*We will just have to wait and see what happens.*
When I got the medicine in me, I haven't looked behind me since.	*The medicine which I took has cured my sickness.*
God love them.	*To feel pity for someone.*
Yer mother is on the war path.	*Your mother is angry.*
I think I got a bit of a raw deal.	*I was treated unfairly.*
That'll all be brushed under the carpet.	*That will be covered up.*
What 'bout ye'?	*How are you?*

It just had to happen at the mouth of Christmas.	*Something (usually bad) which has happened a few days before Christmas.*
Ah Christmas is just another day.	*I can't be bothered with Christmas.*
Is there any word of Christmas with ye?	*Have you started to prepare for Christmas yet?*
Christmas is as far away now as ever.	*This phrase will normally be used on Boxing Day or a few days after Christmas to imply that it is a full year until it happens again.*
We've got our wires crossed.	*We got misunderstood.*
Catch yerself on!	*Behave yourself.*
It's as far out as Tandragee lighthouse.	*Something which is a good distance away or someone who was badly off target.*
That material is that light, ye could spit through it.	*A material which would be easily ripped.*
They've it down to a fine art.	*They are experts at something.*
Ye'd need to beef it up a bit.	*You should increase the size or quantity of something to improve it.*
That place can be hit or miss.	*You can be lucky or unlucky.*
There's no call for the half of it.	*It is not needed.*

They're a blast from the past.	*They have not been heard of for years.*
I don't know how ye stick it.	*I find it hard to believe how you live such a busy / competitive lifestyle.*
They're as common as muck.	*They are ill mannered.*
I worked my socks off.	*I work hard.*
Throwin' the baby out with the bath water.	*I discarded more than what was intended.*
I've seen them in a different light.	*I have seen a new side to them.*
Ye never know who might be earry wiggin'.	*You never know who is listening.*
I was runnin' about like a blue arsc fly.	*Moving around quickly with lots of things to do.*
All over the shop.	*Don't know what you're doing.*
I'm headin' for the Big Smoke.	*I am going to the city.*
You're better with a good prod than a bad catholic.	*Be careful with the company you keep.*
It couldn't have happened to a nicer person.	*It served them right.*
I didn't know what road to look.	*I didn't know how to react.*
I was cut to the bone.	*I was shocked.*

No sweat.	*No problem.*
He put them on their feet.	*He brought a lot of trade to a business or spend a lot of money in the same place.*
That's cat.	*That is terrible.*
There were a lot of rubber-neckers.	*There were nosey people.*
I think I'll hit the scratcher.	*I want to go to bed.*
Ye just can't win.	*You can't get anything right.*
Every day brings its own news.	*Each day brings new information.*
I'm goin' for a skite 'round.	*I'm going out looking for fun.*
I was clean boggin'.	*I was dirty or smelt badly.*
That really takes the biscuit / cake.	*That is astonishing.*
You're only takin' a hand outa me!	*You are trying to fool me!*
When God goes til' the garden he doesn't pick a weed.	*Good people always die young.*
I've no time for them.	*I dislike those people.*
Ye'll soon be six feet under.	*Life is short.*
That man keeps a very rough joint.	*He has a very untidy or dirty house.*

The country is coped.	*Many weird / unusual occurrences that cannot be understood.*
Where's last year's snow?	*Something which has disappeared or no longer exists.*
It is like tryin' to find Holy Water in an Orange hall.	*It is impossible to find.*
Their house is just full of odds an' ends.	*A house full of disparate items.*
Those trousers look like drain pipes on ye.	*Trousers which are too tight on someone.*
Ye can tear away there.	*You get on with it.*
It'd take the light from yer eyes.	*It would surprise you.*
Just goin' through the motions.	*Doing something for the sake of it.*
I'm away to clock.	*I am going to the toilet and I will be a long time.*
He's that straight he's crooked.	*Sticks to the rules to such an extent that it is awkward.*
Ye'd soon get labelled.	*You would soon get a reputation.*
I'm at a loose end.	*I don't know what to do.*
She's never aff the batter, thon doll!	*She is an energetic person.*

I'll be there if God spares me.	*If you are still alive or if God permits, you will attend an event.*
She took a beamer.	*To go red with embarrassment.*
Could ye mind those weins?	*Could you mind the children?*
He must be from the other side of the house or he kicks with the other foot.	*He is from a different religious background.*
I've seen enough to do ma.	*I have had enough.*
Don't worry about me I'm aisy.	*I don't mind one way or the other.*
He'll not break much delft.	*He won't make a difference.*
I'm only coddin' ye.	*I am just teasing you.*
You've a face on ye like a Lurgan spade!	*You look depressed or have a long face.*
I just can't warm 'til them at all.	*I don't like them at all.*
Whatever ye say, say nothin'.	*Be careful what you say.*
He hadn't got a stitch on him / not a ronion on him.	*He was naked.*
I wouldn't know 'er if I met 'er in the street.	*A person who is unfamiliar to you.*
She was dressed to the nineties / nines.	*She was dressed up in fine clothing.*

It went clean outa' ma head.	*I completely forgot about something.*
It's gettin' outa hand.	*Things are getting out of control.*
He'd work the 2 minutes silence.	*He is hard working.*
It'll never get off the ground.	*It will not succeed.*
He's livin' dangerously.	*He is behaving foolishly.*
I completely lost the head with him.	*I was very annoyed with him.*
Leave it well enough alone.	*Do not get involved.*
The luck is hangin' outa him.	*A lucky individual.*
They pulled the rug from under my feet.	*They took away something vital.*
It would never go out of place.	*It will always be there if needed.*
That wall isn't too well built, ye could blow it over.	*That would be easily knocked over.*
I haven't a worry / care in the world.	*I am not worried.*
There could have been a row as big as fight.	*There could have been a huge argument or fight.*
We're just off the boil at the minute.	*When a team has had a few bad performances in a row this expression will be used.*

I'm toilin' with that idea.	*I am considering doing that.*

Under Pressure

I don't know whether I'm comin' or goin'.	*I am really busy and constantly going from one place to another.*
He has been thrown in at the deep end.	*He was not adequately prepared.*
If ye can't stand the heat get outa the kitchen!	*If you can't stand the pressure, go away!*
I've a list of things to do, the length of yer arm.	*I have a long list of things to do.*
That'll lighten the load a bit for me.	*That will help me.*
I haven't put a dent in the work yet.	*I haven't made much progress.*
Up to high doh.	*Worried and stressed.*
It won't be a blink 'til it's over.	*Anything that is going to take place in the near future.*
You've a lot on yer plate at the minute.	*You have a lot to cope with.*
Good job ye came because ye pulled me out of a hole.	*You were very helpful.*
I'm ready for the hills.	*I am stressed out and finding it difficult to cope. I have had enough.*

There are just not enough hours in the day.

You are very busy can't get everything done which you need to.

We've a lot of ground to cover.

We have a lot to do.

I'll soon meet myself comin' back.

I don't understand what I meant to be doing because I'm so busy.

My back is to the wall.

I am in a difficult situation with very little room to manoeuvre.

I feel like pullin' my hair out.

I am under immense pressure.

I'm at my wits end.

To be in despair.

A list the length of your arm.

You've yer hands full.	*You are very busy at present.*
I'm only knockin' my head aff a wall.	*I am trying to do something and it is not working.*
It's a race against the clock.	*You have a certain time limit in order to complete a task.*

Untrustworthy

Ye couldn't trust them as far as ye could throw them.	*They are untrustworthy.*
We think that he might have had a hand in it.	*We believe that he had something to do with it.*
There's a hole in them that ye could drive a bus through.	*Someone you could not trust.*
Ye'd think that butter wouldn't melt in his mouth.	*You would think that he would no wrong.*
They'd steal the eye outa yer head and come back for the socket.	*They are compulsive thieves.*
Ye'd need eyes in the back of yer head when he's about.	*A person who can't be trusted or who has a bad reputation.*
Are ye workin'? Workin' moves would be more like it.	*A manipulative person.*
You're probably gona to tell me a lie anyway.	*You have a reputation for being untruthful.*
I wouldn't put it past ye.	*I think you would do it.*

Ye need to keep a close eye on them because ye couldn't watch 'em.	*A person you don't trust at all and you feel the need to watch them closely.*
They're too hairy to be fairy.	*People that are untrustworthy.*
He'd lift it from under yer nose.	*He is an outrageous thief.*
Ye'd need to sleep with one eye open with him about.	*A person that you couldn't trust and who you would need to watch carefully.*
He's just leadin' ye down the garden path.	*To give a person false information which causes them to waste their time.*
Ye shouldn't tar them all with the same brush.	*You shouldn't have the same opinion of them all.*
They're as fly as a fox.	*A cunning person who does things to better themselves in whatever way possible.*
That man would take the teeth out of a saw.	*A person who you cannot trust as they have been known to steal things regularly.*
Watch what ye say 'round them or it'll be home before ye.	*You need to be careful who you share information.*
They've more sides than a 50p coin.	*They are inconsistent.*

Hurry Up

Ye may give yerself a bit of shake.	*You need to hurry up.*
Ye may get yer finger out.	*Get on with what needs to be done.*
Ye may get yer arse in gear.	*You should hurry up and get organised.*
Ye may get a move on.	*You need to make a start at the task you have been set.*
Ye may get yer skates on.	*Used when you want to tell someone to hurry up.*
Don't be dilly dallin'.	*Stop messing around.*

Lazy people

They're just lyin' there like a couch potato.	*A lazy person.*
There isn't a turn in 'em.	*They wouldn't help anyone.*
You're sittin' up there like a big lump of lard / a Lord.	*You are very lazy and useless.*
Do ye get up a wee while every day?	*Do you like to spend a long time lying in bed?*
He wouldn't walk outa yer road.	*An individual find the easiest tasks a chore.*
Ye wouldn't scratch yerself if ye were itchy.	*A lazy person that would not do anything for themselves.*

If work was in bed ye'd lie under it.	*Someone who rarely ever does any work.*
You're lyin' up there like a big beach whale.	*Lying on a seat in a way that resembles that of a whale when it is on the beach.*
He's that lazy that the dead lice are fallin' off him.	*He is a very lazy person.*
He'd sleep the clock 'round.	*He would sleep all day.*
They haven't done a tap all day.	*They have done nothing.*

In trouble

Someone must have blown the whistle on him.	*Someone must have told on him.*
He hasn't a leg to stand on.	*There is a lot of evidence to suggest that he did something wrong.*
Someone will have to take the rap for it.	*Someone will get blamed for it.*
They've been stitched up and they'll be headin' for the clink.	*They have been set up and now they have to go to jail.*

Smart / clever people

He knows every trick in the book.	*A person who uses dishonest or clever ways to achieve what they want.*

They'll be reelin' them in.	*Taking in a large quantity of something usually money or it can also be people.*
He has them wrapped 'round his wee finger.	*When a person knows how to control someone else in order to get them to do what they want.*
He wouldn't travel far with a stone in his shoe.	*When you know something is not right, you would not go ahead with it.*
She'll not get lost anyway.	*She is sensible.*
They know what side his bread is buttered on anyway.	*Someone who understands not to act in way that would lose them other people's approval.*
He wouldn't be at a hole that there was no mouse in.	*Someone who wouldn't do something unless they were going to benefit from it financially.*
He'll not sell his hen 'til a rainy day.	*He will not sell something until he is getting the very best price for it.*
They'd leave ye high an' dry.	*To leave someone in a difficult situation which they have no way of making it better.*

Chapter 9
The Weather

It's rainin' cats and dogs

I'll be there rain, hail or snow.	*I will be there no matter what the weather is like.*
It was howlin' like a banshee.	*The wind was whistling and making a lot of noise.*
The sun was splittin' the trees.	*A lovely spell of sunshine.*
It's a quare an' close evenin'.	*A warm or humid evening.*
Ye wouldn't put a milk bottle out in that weather.	*The weather is really bad.*
It's fairly startin' to drop down at night.	*It is getting darker each evening.*
The evenings are away with it.	*The nights are becoming darker.*
That weather would sicken ye!	*The weather is really getting on your nerves.*
It's a dirty ole day.	*The weather isn't great and it would get you down.*
The road is that slippy it's just like a bottle.	*Bottles / glasses have a shiny surface which is slippy, so this refers to a road which is covered in ice.*
Ye should make hay while the sun shines.	*Make the most of opportunities while you can.*
Red sky at night, a shepherd's delight.	*A red sky normally indicates that the weather will be good the following day.*

Red sky in the mornin', sailors warnin'.	*Indicates bad or rough seas.*
It'll not be long 'til the turn of the day.	*Spring is known as the 'turn of the day' when the weather starts to get slightly warmer and the plants begin to grow.*
Cold hands, warm heart.	*Just because a person's hands are cold doesn't mean they aren't a good person.*
Ye couldn't have seen yer finger in front of ye.	*The visibility was poor due to the bad weather.*
It's a fox of a day.	*You are not aware of what the weather will be like.*
We are gettin' all the seasons in one day.	*Very changeable weather.*
The Lord is playin' his drums.	*Usually said when there is thunder around.*
Clear moon, frost soon.	*A full moon in a cloudless sky usually indicates that frost is on its way.*
That's the weather now.	*To state that you like the weather in recent days.*
The month came in like a lamb an' out like a lion.	*The weather at the beginning of the month was fine but towards the end of the month it was extremely bad.*
There isn't an air that night.	*A very still / calm night.*

That day doesn't know what to do.

Very changeable weather, one minute it is raining and the next minute the sun is shining.

The Wet

The heavens have opened.

There was a sudden shower of heavy rain.

It's comin' down like stair rods.

Rain which is coming down at an extremely fast rate.

I see the sky startin' to close in.

It is beginning to cloud over.

A rainy day isn't a day for children.

If it is raining children will play indoors and annoy their parents.

It's rainin' cats an' dogs.

It is raining heavily and the drops of rain are huge.

Ah it's only a bit of a skift.

There has only been a little shower of rain.

It's bucketin' outa da heavens.

It is raining heavily.

The rain was beltin' aff the windows.

The rain was pounding off the windows and making a lot of noise.

It's not takin' time to come down.

The rain was coming down very fast.

They're just like drowned rats.

They are extremely wet.

It's some day for the ducks.	*A wet day is a great day for ducks because they enjoy swimming in the water.*
I'm wet through to the skin.	*My clothes are completely soaked and I can feel the damp against my skin.*
God has turned on the water tap.	*It has begun to rain.*
She has as many wrinkles on 'er face that would hold a fortnight's rain.	*Describes a person with an old and wrinky face.*

The Cold

The wind is so cold the day, it would cut ye in two.	*A cold wind which is very 'sharp'.*
It's bitter cold the day.	*It is an extremely cold day which causes an unpleasant, painful or stinging sensation on your skin.*
You're like the weather anyway.	*Someone who is wearing many coats as if they were experiencing bad weather.*
It would founder ye.	*It is freezing cold.*
The wind would cut the horns off a snail.	*There is a very cold wind.*
It's a sharp mornin'.	*The temperature is low today.*

I hope that we don't get the weather you're expectin' anyway!

Someone who is wearing many layers of clothing in good weather.

It'd clean corn out there.

An extremely cold day.

Ye'd catch yer death out in that weather.

The weather is so bad that if you stayed out in it long enough, you could die from the cold.

It was so cold that it would have made yer glass eye water.

It is an extremely cold day.

I can't get the heat into ma.

I can't seem to get warm.

It'd skin ye.

It is freezing cold and there is a sharp wind.

There's not a lot of heat about.

It's not warm at all.

My nipples were that cold, they were like bullets.

My nipples have become prominent due to the cold.

It's makin' me cold lookin' at ye.

Someone who is shivering with the cold and they are wearing a lot of clothes. You actually seem to feel like you are cold as well.

That's a hardy mornin'.

It is a cold morning.

It'd freeze the balls off a brass monkey.

An extremely cold day.

Chapter 10
Love & Relationships

She's goin' to be left on the shelf.

They say that a bad dog kills at home.	*Someone going out with a local person or it can also mean to commit a crime in your own community.*
There's no point in havin' a cage an' no bird to put in it.	*There is little point having a house if you do not have a partner to live with.*
You're like a dog chasin' a bus an' if ye caught it ye wouldn't know how to ride it.	*Someone who you have no chance of going out with but whom you pursue regardless.*
He swept me off my feet.	*I fell for him immediately.*
She just gave me the cold shoulder.	*She was unfriendly.*
They're a match made in heaven.	*They are a perfect match for each other.*
She's a lot of baggage with 'er.	*She has children / many problems or both.*
They've stuck together through thick an' thin.	*They have stayed together in good and bad times.*
Ye can look at the menu but ye don't have te order.	*You can look at other boys / girls even if you already have a partner but you don't have to go out with them.*
Some people live in each other's shadows.	*Some people are inseparable.*
They've grown on me.	*They improve on acquaintship.*

She wears the trousers in that relationship anyway.	*She is in control of what goes on in the relationship.*
If ye were sent out blindfolded, ye couldn't have come back with worse.	*You have made a bad choice.*
She's goin' to be left on the shelf.	*She is old and is not going to meet a partner.*
Well, if he can get a woman then there's hope for the rest of us.	*An ugly person who you never thought would get a partner has recently become attached.*
She's been around a few corners.	*She has had many different partners.*
That pair are like beauty an' the beast.	*A couple where one is beautiful and the other is ugly.*
Ye couldn't pull weeds.	*You could not get yourself an attractive partner or you can't do anything.*
He has 'er on a tight lead.	*He controls her.*
There's many a good tune played on an ole fiddle.	*Older people are as capable as younger ones are.*
She's that ugly, not even a sniper would take 'er out.	*An ugly individual who no one would even consider taking out on a date.*
He's doin' a big line at the minute.	*He is in a serious relationship.*
I wouldn't see them in my soup.	*I am not attracted to them.*

I wouldn't take ye to the back door.	*I really dislike you.*
Don't rest yer eyes beyond what's yer own.	*Don't look at another man's wife.*
She just dropped him like a hot knife.	*She left her partner extremely quickly.*
Ye must have had the beer goggles on when ye picked them.	*You must have been drunk when you choose him / her.*
She has 'er work cut out with 'im.	*He is different to control.*
The chase is always better than the catch.	*Trying to get out with someone can be more exciting than actually being with someone.*
Ye'd swear that those two were joined at the hip.	*Two people who are inseparable.*
Ye never see one without the other.	*Constant companions.*
She's put 'er foot down / boot down.	*To tell someone that they must do or stop doing something immediately.*
I wouldn't see ye in ma road.	*I wouldn't be bothered with you.*
She's only with him for the money.	*A person who is only with their partner because they are wealthy.*

She's a gold digger.	*Someone who does not have any feelings for their partner they are only with them for their money.*
He was holdin' on til' 'er like a new shade.	*Staying very close to someone who you have only met recently.*
What's yours is mine an' what's mine is my own.	*This statement means that your partner does not intend to share anything with you.*
They've been goin' out since Adam was a boy.	*A couple that has been together for a very long time.*
There's always a good woman behind every good man.	*A man always needs a woman or partner to support him in whatever way possible.*
True love never dies.	*If you truly love someone this will always stay with you whereas lust fades away over time.*
Absence makes the heart grow fonder.	*Our affection increases when we are away from our loved ones.*
Love is blind.	*Love can make you ignore problems or the appearance of the person who you are with.*
Opposites attract.	*Two people who are the complete opposite to each other will often end up together.*

Older men make better lovers.

Older men may show you more love than younger men as they are more mature.

Attraction to the opposite sex

Ye wouldn't throw 'er outa bed for fartin' anyway.

You can accept anything she does because she is beautiful.

She's a quare bit of stuff.

She is a good looking girl.

He's like a dog in heat.

He is a sex maniac.

There's a spark between them.

There is chemistry between them.

You're a bit of a rake!

You are someone who has numerous partners.

She doesn't leave much to the imagination.

She hasn't many clothes on.

Yeah ye would.

You would kiss a certain person, as you think they are handsome looking.

They've a woman at every port.

A person who tends to have many different partners in all areas of the country.

No point in lookin' at somethin' ye can't have.

There is no point looking at a person that you have no chance with.

I suppose ye could do worse.

You are satisfied that someone's partner isn't too bad looking.

Arguin' & break-ups

There's plenty more fish in the sea.

There is plenty more people in the world.

I've been burnt before an' I don't want to get burnt again.

I am not prepared to suffer in the same way twice.

There are always three sides to a story, his, hers and the truth.

One person will have their version of a story, then there is their partner's version and the truth which is usually different from both versions.

I'll wash my hands of him.

I will ignore him and get him out of my life.

They fight like cat an' dog.

Two people who are constantly fighting.

I can't do with ye an' I couldn't do without ye.

I don't like you but I wouldn't be without you.

There're as many good fish in the sea as ever came out of it.

There are plenty of people in the world to suit you.

I'll be in the dog house when I get home.

I will be in trouble when you get home.

If its abuse ye want get married.

If you want to fight get married.

An ole fire is easy lit.

Old relationships are easily returned.

They'll be at each other's throats.

They will be argumentative or fight with each other.

Marriage

I used to have money, an' then I got married!	*I felt rich then I got married and now I have little money.*
The only cure for love is marriage.	*Love is like a disease, it takes a grip on you so when you love someone dearly then you should marry them.*
When are ye goin' to pop the question?	*When are you going to propose.*
Have a good forenoon because it could be a long afternoon.	*Enjoy yourself before you are married because you might not be able to do it when you are older.*
When ye get married, yer heart is in yer mouth an' yer hand is in yer pocket.	*Before you get married you may have been more care free with not a worry in the world and spent a lot less money.*
We went before the whistle or went without the license.	*To have a child before you are married.*
It's 'bot time I put up my own smoke.	*I am ready to settle down and start my own family.*
We are goin' to try before we buy.	*We are going to try living together before getting married.*
It's about time you were off the road.	*You need to settle down and get married.*

Chapter 11

Money & Wealth

Do you think the money is goin' to come out of the sky?

I'd see them in hell before I'd give them that sort of money.	*I refuse to give them so much money.*
Where do ye think the money is goin' to come from, outa the sky?	*Money does not just appear out of nowhere, it has to be earned and is not easy to come by.*
He'd go through money as if it was goin' out fashion.	*He spends money at an exceptionally fast rate.*
Ye get what ye pay for.	*Normally cheap items will not be good quality and won't last long.*
Penny wise an' pound foolish.	*Those who save small sums of money but spend large amounts of money regularly.*
I'll have to rob the piggy bank to get the money for that.	*I will have to use some of my savings in order to pay for something.*
It's only money for ole rope.	*An easy way of making money.*
A fair exchange is no robbery.	*Swapping one thing for another fairly with someone cannot be regarded as stealing.*
Not for love nor love.	*I would not do that regardless of the money being offered.*
I wouldn't take a pension to do that.	*If I was offered money for the rest of my life I still wouldn't do that.*

If ye pay peanuts, ye get monkeys.	*If you pay low wages to your employees will only get those people who are not as intelligent or skilled.*
Young an' foolish.	*Young people don't have much experience and do foolish things with their money.*
Money talks.	*When you are wealthy people are more likely to listen to you.*
A fool and his money are easily parted.	*Refers to those people who aren't careful with their money and spend it without thinking.*
They say that money follows money or money goes to money.	*If your family or relatives have money then usually you will have money.*
Ye might as well throw yer money in the fire / throw it over the hedge.	*To waste or mismanage your money.*
If I had a pound for every time I've heard that I'd be a rich man now.	*I have been told something many, many times.*
Whatever I owe ye is not worth talkin' about.	*I owe you a very small amount of money.*
Some businesses find it hard to stay afloat.	*Managing the cash flow in a business is one of the most difficult things and it is for this reason many businesses end up going bankrupt.*

They'd give ye the last penny they had in their pocket.

Kind people who would offer you money even if they had very little money themselves.

Ye only get a lend of it.

You don't seem to have money for very long before you have to spend it again.

He could sell snow to the Eskimo's.

He is good at selling things.

Talk is cheap but it takes money to buy drink.

It is easy to talk about what you will buy but it's harder when you have to actually spend your money.

I'll pay ye for that on the drip.

I will pay that back in installments.

Ye may put that on the slate for me.

You can add that to what I already owe you and I will pay you at a later date.

It's about time ye coughed up the money.

It is about time you paid the money you owe.

Money doesn't buy happiness.

You could have all the money in the world but you might not actually be happy.

A car / girlfriend are like a money box with no bottom in it.

A car or a girlfriend are expensive things to keep as you are constantly buying things for them.

That shop is a complete gold mine.

A business which is making a lot of money.

All the money in the world will not make a racehorse from an ass.	*It wouldn't matter how much money you spend trying to improve something, if it's not good quality to begin with.*
How much did that set ye back?	*How much did that cost you?*
Time is money.	*Most people are paid per hour so the more time you spend not working the less you earn.*
Rob Peter to pay Paul.	*You have to borrow money from a person / organisation to pay another.*
I'll get ye again.	*You can pay the money you owe me another time.*
Cut yer coat accordin' to yer cloth.	*Only buy what you have the money to pay for, otherwise you will get yourself into debt.*
That thing is not worth 2D.	*When something holds worth very little value.*
Everythin' they touch turns to gold.	*They can make money from anything.*
He knows the price of everythin' an' the value of nothin'.	*He who knows the cost of everything but doesn't understand the value of money.*
A debt is still a debt even if forgotten.	*If you owe a person a sum of money you should always pay them even if they have forgotten about it.*

He, who pays the piper, calls the tune.

If you pay for someone's services, then you can decide what you want them to do.

I wouldn't take a million pounds to do that.

It wouldn't matter how much money someone offered me to do a task, it wouldn't be enough.

It's good to have a bit behind ye.

It is advisble to save money encase you need it.

Would ye take a bad price for that?

Are you willing to offer someone a small sum of money for an item?

I'll give ye a run for yer money.

I believe that I could beat you at a competition or in a bet.

That doesn't owe me anythin' anyway.

Something which has earned you a lot of money and paid for itself.

Another day, another dollar.

You treat each day as if it is just another opportunity to earn money.

Money talks all languages.

Even if people don't speak the same language they can still understand money.

I'm startin' to feel the pinch.

I am beginning to have problems managing my money because I have less than I used to.

No mon, no fun.

You can't enjoy yourself without having money.

Bribery can split a stone.	*Money can get you anything.*
In for a penny in for a pound.	*If you are going to take a risk you might as well as take a big risk.*
Never reach yer hand further than ye can withdraw it.	*Do not give too much of your money away or you will get into difficulty.*
Will it even wash it's face?	*Will a project cover its expenses?*
There's money in muck.	*You can make money from anything.*
That's my bread an' butter.	*That is how I earn my living and depend on.*
It might not wash it's face.	*It might not make a profit or cover the expenses.*
Pickings are light.	*There isn't much food / money around.*
It's worth the full of yer arse of boiled gooseberries.	*It is worthless.*
That man would sell the shirt aff his back.	*He would sell anything belonging to him if someone offered them money.*
Never refuse money.	*If someone offers you money take it.*
It'll take somethin' to put that over.	*A function / event will cost a lot of money.*

Money is the root of all evil.	*Money is the main cause of all the crime and badness that exists in the world.*
Money is like muck, no use unless its spread.	*Money seems much more enjoyable when it's spent and many different people get the benefit of it.*
Money doesn't grow on trees.	*You have to work to earn money; it doesn't come easily or without effort.*

Cheats

Ye must have paid yer way there.	*You have got into somewhere illegally by giving someone a bribe.*
They're always lookin' somethin' for nothin'.	*They always want things from you for free.*
He's only in it to see what he can get outa it.	*He is only involved to receive the benefits.*
Give a little an' promise a lot.	*A person who pays you a little amount of money and promises to give you more.*
They could buy an' sell ye in a minute.	*They know how to use a certain language or manner in order to buy or sell something to you.*
I would say he got a brave handshake out of it.	*I believe that he was paid a substantial sum of money for doing something.*

Them one's would fleece ye.	*Those who charge extortionate prices for their goods.*
He's just linin' his pockets.	*He receives too much money or money which was not intended for them.*
They'd soon wipe yer eye.	*Dishonest people who would trick you into thinking something was worth more than it actually was.*
It's all about beatin' the system if ye can.	*Pay as little tax as possible and avoid any extra charges.*

Money doesn't grow on trees

They'll be lookin' an arm an' a leg for it.

They ask for an extremely high price for an item.

It was sold under the table.

It was sold quietly, without any publicity.

He wouldn't pay attention, never mind any of his bills.

He doesn't pay his bills.

That cheque isn't worth the paper that it's written on.

That cheque is absolutely worthless.

It's bare faced / daylight robbery.

Someone who has blatantly overcharged you for an object.

They'd put the arm into ye til' the elbow.

They would charge you extortionate prices for a product or service.

The hungry eye sees far.

When people are looking for something in particular they can spot in among other things.

It was sold out the back door.

It was sold without many knowing it was for sell and for less than its market value.

Miserable people

It's better to spend money like there's no th'mara than to spend tonight like there's no money.

It is better to spend the money you have rather than going through life as if you have no money.

Ye'd need a gun to get money outa them.

They do not like to pay anyone.

If he owned Switzerland he wouldn't even give ye a slide.	*He wouldn't share with you or give you anything he owns.*
He wouldn't give his mother a glass of water if she was dyin'.	*A greedy person / he will not share with anyone.*
They wouldn't spend Christmas.	*They do not like to buy anything for anyone.*
I don't know why he's holdin' on til' his money because he can't take it with him.	*I think there is little point in saving your money up all your life because you can't take it with you when you die.*
Every pound / penny is a prisoner.	*Those who never spend any of their money as soon as they get it they keep it.*
As tight as a camel's arse in a sandstorm / as tight as a duck's arse in water.	*A person who would not or does not like to spend money at all.*
He wouldn't spend daylight.	*He doesn't like to spend any money.*
They wouldn't give ye the time of day.	*They wouldn't give you anything belonging to them.*
It's like tryin' to get blood out of a stone.	*It is impossible to get money from them.*
He wouldn't give ye the steam of his piss.	*He wouldn't give you anything.*
They still have their communion money.	*Those who do not like to spend their money and would rather save it.*

Ye wouldn't think that they hadn't an arse in their trousers.	*You would not think they are wealthy because they do not buy expensive items and they dress like they do not have much money.*
He came to the party with his two arms the one length.	*He arrived at a venue with nothing to give the host as a gift.*
Ye'll only get the breathe of his back anyway or 6ft will hold them.	*Usually said when someone charges people a lot of money or who constantly fights with people over money or land.*
He could peel an orange in his pocket for fear of ye seein' it.	*He wouldn't want you to see what money he has incase you might ask them for some of it.*
Ye'll not break the bank anyway.	*You will not spend much money on anything.*
That family is as miserable as sin.	*That family does not like to spend any money at all.*

Poor people

I can't seem to get my head above water.	*I am finding it hard to get out of debt.*
He's in debt til' the neck.	*He is in a lot of debt.*
They haven't got a penny to their name.	*They have no money at all.*
If I had any money, I'd frame it.	*I have no money, but if I did I would hang onto it.*

She has a fur coat an' no knickers.	*A woman who is draped in expensive clothing or other accessories, but who don't have much money.*
Money always seems to go in one hand an' out the other.	*Each time you earn some money, it has to go towards paying bills.*
They wouldn't have two pennies to rub together.	*To have little or no money at all.*
Keep the wolf from the door.	*To have enough money to be able to eat and live.*
I haven't a bean on ma / I'm skint.	*I have not got any money on me at all.*
They are going to go down the tube.	*They are going to go bankrupt.*

Filthy rich people

Some people don't mind havin' to pay through the nose for somethin'.	*Some people are happy to pay a lot of money for an item even if it is not worth it.*
He always carries a wad of notes in his pocket that would choke an elephant.	*He carries a large bundle of cash in their pocket.*
They must have money to burn.	*They spend a lot of money on things which are not necessary.*
The money must be burnin' a hole in their pocket.	*Those people who cannot wait to get spending money.*

He's well to do.

He has a good job and is wealthy.

I don't know where they're gettin' all that money they must be printin' it.

Someone who always seems to have a lot of cash and you don't know where they are getting it from.

They have that much money that they don't know what to do with it.

They have so much money that they find it hard to spend.

Ye can't hide money.

When you are wealthy you can buy a lot of expensive items then people know that you have money.

Money is no object.

Those people who do not care how much something costs.

He wouldn't be short of a pound.

He has plenty of money.

They spend money like water

They spend money rapidly.

A heavy purse makes a light heart.

When you have plenty of money, you feel happy and secure in life.

I wish I was a pound behind them.

If I was a pound behind them I would have a lot of money.

He has as much money as would sink a ship.

He has plenty of money.

Chapter 12

Eatin' & Drinkin'

He has been holdin' the bar up all night.

Food

I wouldn't feed that food to the dog.	*Poor quality food which tastes disgusting.*
She eats nothin', a pigeon would eat more.	*She eats very little food*
I'm that hungry, I could eat a horse.	*I could eat a large meal.*
There must have been a mouse in our fridge.	*Someone has tasted something without eating the rest of it.*
It'll put hairs on yer chest like bull wire.	*It will make you strong.*
That's me fed an' watered.	*I have had enough to eat and drink.*
Fred! There's no bread.	*A way to telling someone that you need to buy some bread.*
Horse it into ye!	*Eat up quickly.*
Ye'd think ye hadn't seen food this week or more.	*You would think that you were starving.*
What do ye think I am? A bin?	*I really can't eat anymore!*
He got stuck into the dinner like a day's work.	*He ate quickly.*
Those peas are that hard they're like bullets.	*Peas which are not cooked properly making them hard to chew.*

There's not a bite in the house.	*There is no food left.*
They'd eat ye outa house an' home.	*They've have great appetites.*
My belly thinks my throat is cut.	*I am starving.*
I'm 'atin' on the wing.	*'Eating on the wing' means taking fast food or eating as you go.*
Ye couldn't boil an egg.	*You can't cook.*
They've an awful sweet tooth.	*They like a lot of sweet things.*
What the eye doesn't see, the stomach doesn't grieve over.	*If you haven't seen any nice food then you won't want it as much.*
Ye are what ye eat!	*If you eat healthy foods then you will be healthy but if you eat fatty foods you'll be obese.*
A full stomach never thinks of an empty one.	*Someone who has already eaten won't care about someone that hasn't.*
I like cabbage but cabbage doesn't like me.	*I like the taste of cabbage but it is hard to digest.*
First to the pot an' last to work.	*An individual who prefers food to work.*
Yer eyes are bigger than yer belly.	*You got more food than you could eat.*

I wouldn't give ye anythin' that I wouldn't ate myself.

I would only treat you like I do myself.

I'm as full as a tick.

I am extremely full after eating a meal.

That food turned my stomach.

That food was unappetising and made me feel sick.

Ye'd think that ye had never seen food before.

Eating your food quickly without taking the time to chew it properly.

The way to a man's heart is through his belly.

If you want to win over a man, give him plenty of nice food.

I didn't know whether to eat it or climb it.

A really large meal which is piled up high on the plate.

Drink

Ye may open that door, the tea is weak!

Refers to weak tea which is very light in colour.

This tea is that strong that ye stand on it.

Tea which is very dark in colour.

Ye wouldn't wet that tea.

To pour water from the kettle into the teapot.

The tea was like dishwater.

Weak or lightly coloured tea.

They wouldn't ask ye if ye had a mouth on ye.

They wouldn't offer you a drink.

I'll have to wet my whistle.

I will have to take a drink.

Over eatin'

If ye eat anymore of that cake ye'll swell up like a poisoned pup.	*If you eat too much food and your stomach will swell up.*
I'd rather keep ye a week, as to a month!	*I would not like to feed you for any period of time.*
I ate a feed that would have kilt a horse.	*To eat a large quantity of food.*
Ye'd eat all that is put in front of ye.	*You have a good appetite.*
I'm that full I'm about to burst.	*I have overeaten and to feel like I am going to be sick.*
They weren't fit to move an inch.	*They ate so much food that they can hardly move.*
If he eats anymore of them he'll turn into one.	*He eats large quantities of the same food.*
I'm as full as a sheugh.	*I'm full up of food or alcohol.*
Ye'd think that she had worms.	*She never stops eating.*
I'm only after eatin' a whole rake of stuff.	*I ate a lot of different food dishes a short time ago.*
After I had eaten my dinner, I was ful' 'til the neck.	*I am full up and couldn't eat anymore food.*
Ye don't eat 'til yer full ye eat 'til yer tired.	*You do not know when to stop eating.*

A fat Christmas makes for a tight graveyard.	*Over-eating at Christmas time causes weight gain which eventually could lead to death.*
I was that full I wasn't fit to fart.	*I have eaten too much food and I can hardly move.*

Alcohol & bein' drunk

Take the hair of the dog that bit ye.	*To take a small amount of alcohol when you are hung over and are trying to recover.*
The truth comes out when the spirits are in.	*People share their true feelings about someone or disclose information when they're drunk.*
She's half tore.	*She is drunk.*
He's been standin' there all night holdin' the bar up.	*He has stood beside the bar all night drinking.*
We met through drink.	*We met on a night out in a pub.*
I'll drink ye under the table.	*My alcohol tolerance is better than yours.*
It'd take paint off a door.	*Extremely strong alcohol.*
Their breathe smelt like a brewery or ye would get drunk on their breath.	*Bad breath due to consuming a lot of alcohol.*

He drinks like a camel.	*He is an alcoholic.*
I'll have to go to the pub because there's an awful drooth on ma!	*I am thirsty so I am going for a pint!*
You're only a wee lightweight.	*It does not take much alcohol to get you drunk.*
I need somethin' to wet my lips!	*I need a pint!*
They'd drive ye to the drink.	*They are annoying.*
He was as drunk as a Lord.	*He was highly intoxicated.*
Watch ye don't fall into that.	*Usually said to a small person who is sitting over a large drink normally a pint of beer or it could be a trap.*
He's drunk a farm of land, the tractor and the house.	*He has spent all the money he had on alcohol.*
He'd drink the river dry.	*He consumes vast quantities of alcohol.*
They've put away some drink.	*They drank a large amount of alcohol.*
You're lookin' a bit worse for wear.	*You look poorly.*
I wasn't fit to bit my finger.	*Completely drunk.*
We're goin' to drown the shamrock.	*We are going to drink and celebrate St. Paddy's Day.*

My mouth is that dry I couldn't even spit or it was as dry as Gandy's flip flop.	*My mouth is suffering due to the after affect's of a night out on the beer.*
He couldn't drink chicken soup.	*He gets drunk with only a small amount of alcohol.*
She was that drunk, she was talkin' like a washin' machine.	*She was not making any sense / mispronouncing her words.*
We'll have te wet the baby's head.	*Drink to the baby's health.*
That would put yer light out.	*A strong alcoholic drink that could get you drunk easily.*
They'd be fond of a drop?	*They like to drink alcohol.*
Did ye get a drop?	*Did you get some alcohol?*
You're like the kettle you're steamin' all the time.	*Someone who tends to be drunk most of the time.*
He's that fond of the drink that he'd drink it outa the sheugh.	*He consumes a large quantity of alcohol and would drink it out of anything.*
Alcohol's the root of all evil.	*Alcohol is the main cause of people's problems and it does not solve anything.*
I'm clean dyin' today after last night.	*I am suffering the effects of alcohol.*

Chapter 13
Well Known Sayings

Stop tryin' to put words in my mouth

It's not the end of the world if it does happen.	*Don't worry about something because it is nothing which is so serious that it cannot be fixed.*
God made time, but man-made haste.	*God created the world and time but people always seem to be in a hurry.*
Get down on yer knees an' thank god that you're still on yer feet.	*You should thank God that you are fit and healthy.*
It's all nip and tuck / tip for tot.	*A close contest where the lead keeps shifting from one person or team to another.*
A leopard never loses its spots.	*If someone has done something wrong in the past then they will more than likely do it again in the future.*
They'll only take the cream of the crop.	*The best will always be selected.*
It's a small world.	*If you meet a new person in another country and they know someone who lives near you or they are actually related to someone you know.*
He's got the whole world at his feet.	*He is extremely successful and admired by a great number of people.*
First past the post is the winner.	*The first person to do something will be the winner.*

One step forward and two back.	*You seem to be progressing well with something, but then you hit a few problems and you are set back further than you were when you began.*
It takes time to build castles.	*Something which is complicated or impressive can take a long time to make.*
There's nothin' like blowin' yer own trumpet.	*To boost or praise yourself constantly to others.*
You're only prolongin' the punishment.	*You are only making a problem you have last longer.*
I'll have them eatin' out of the palm of my hand.	*I will have them doing exactly what I want them to do.*
It'll just be in one ear an' out the other.	*Those who don't seem to listen to what you say.*
I was pipped at the post.	*I was beaten at the very last minute in a race or competition.*
Ye need to get the rub of the green.	*You always need luck on your side if you want to win anything.*
I thought I had it in the bag.	*You thought you had won a competition easily, but you were beaten to your surprise.*
When push comes to shove.	*When a situation starts to become more intense or difficult.*

The sky's the limit

There is no limit to the possibilities something or someone could have.

It could make him or break him.

It could go well for him or it could horribly wrong.

I'm suited an' booted.

I am fully dressed in a suit and shoes.

Ye wouldn't do that to yer own flesh an' blood.

You would not do that to your own family or relations.

When the chips are down, ye need to muck in.

When the pressure is being applied everyone needs to help out.

What's good for one is good for them all.

If something is good enough for one person it should be good enough for everyone.

Children should be seen an' not heard.

Children should be quiet and not speak in the presence of adults.

It's just an accident waitin' to happen or it's just a tickin' time bomb.

Something which will more than likely go wrong in the near future.

We'll just have to take it one step at a time.

To deal with things as they happen and don't worry about the future.

Ye might as well chance yer arm.

To risk something might which not work out.

It's either a feast or a famine in 'ere.

There is either too much or not enough of something.

I'm in it to win it.	*I am involved in a competition or task where my main objective is to win.*
It'd take a tear from a stone.	*A very sad occasion or situations which would make anyone cry.*
What fills the eye fills the heart.	*Whatever you feel emotional about means a lot to you and is close to your heart.*
Don't let yer heart know what yer head is thinkin'.	*Always listen to your heart before your head as your head might think about doing things which you would not do in your heart.*
It's all downhill from 'ere on.	*Things will start to become much easier from now on.*
After all's said an' done, more will be said than done.	*People tend to talk a lot about what they intend to do but they never actually do that much.*
Keep yer cards close to yer chest.	*To be very secretive about your intended actions.*
The world is ill-divided.	*One half of the world are rich and have a great quality of life while the other half is poor, with no money and a bad quality of life.*
You're drivin' more nails in the coffin.	*You are just making things worse than they are already are.*

I'm goin' to call it a day.	*I am going to finish something or go to bed soon.*
It's not set in stone.	*Anything which is not 100% certain.*
When ye play with fire, ye'll get burnt.	*If you become involved in dangerous or illegal activities you may get into trouble.*
He never misses a trick.	*A person who sees and hears everything.*
You've only scratched the surface.	*You only discover or deal with a very small part of a problem.*
Give them wings an' let them fly.	*You have to give your offspring the freedom to do what they want or travel where they wish.*
A drownin' man will clutch at a straw.	*When you are desperate, you will look for anything that might help you.*
Oil and water don't mix.	*Certain qualities or personalities are incompatible.*
Still water runs deep.	*People, who are calm and tranquil on the outside, often have a strong, 'deep' personality.*
There's no fool like an old fool.	*Old people are meant to be wise and act appropriately but when they behave foolishly it is worse than a young person.*

Third time lucky.	*You have tried something twice and it didn't work, so it will usually work on the third time.*
Time flies when you're havin' fun.	*When you are enjoying yourself you never realise how much time has went past.*
Two blacks don't make a white / two wrongs don't make a right.	*Faults are not excused by the faults of somebody else.*
What the eye doesn't see, the heart doesn't grieve over.	*If you don't see something happening then you are less likely to be worried or annoyed about it.*
I'm not gettin' a fair crack of the wipe.	*I am not receiving the same opportunities or treatment which others are.*
Kill one, warn a thousand.	*It's better that something bad happen to one person so it means many more people know to be careful.*
No wind, no waves.	*When a wind blows waves occur so therefore only when there is a push, things will happen.*
Time waits for no man.	*No one is powerful enough to stop time; it will always go on no matter what.*
She makes a better friend than an enemy.	*I would rather be on good terms with her than bad. .*

It's all over bar the shoutin'.

This phrase will he used when the result of an event or situation is certain.

Live an' let live.

Let other people do as they please and they will leave you alone.

Never do things by halves.

Always complete the tasks which were given to you.

Mockin' is catchin'.

Be careful not to criticise others who are less fortunate because the same thing could happen to you.

I heard it on the grape vine.

I heard a piece of information from an informal source.

You've got to do yer own growin' no matter how tall yer grandfather was.

It doesn't matter who came before you. You still have to grow up for yourself.

It's goin' like clockwork.

Something which happens at regular times and without any problems.

Christmas has come early.

Something good has happened to you.

They're all jumpin' on the band wagon.

People who start to do something because other people are doing it.

People are comin' out of the woodwork.

Those people who appear unexpectedly or suddenly after being hidden or not active for a long time.

If ye commit the crime ye do the time.	*If you commit a crime you must be prepared for the consequences if you're caught.*
We're tryin' to build bridges between them.	*To resolve differences people have between each other.*
It's a bridge too far.	*An act of overreaching or taking something too far.*
What goes up must come down.	*If something has happened before then it will happen again.*
It was burnt to a crisp.	*It was completely burnt with no moisture left.*
They have itchy feet.	*They do not want to stay in the same place.*
If you've got it flaunt it.	*If you are good looking you might as well show yourself off to others.*
If ye fell in the river, ye'd come out dry.	*You are a lucky person who always seems to be OK no matter what happens to them.*
You're like a fish out of water.	*You seem confused or unhappy with your surroundings.*
It's no skin off my nose.	*The problem is no concern to you and the task is not difficult for you.*
All hell broke loose.	*There was huge confusion or even a fight which started.*

I'm goin' to throw my hat into the ring.	*I am going to enter a political race as a candidate for office.*
Stop tryin' to put words in my mouth.	*When someone tries to persuade you to agree to something or say what they would like to hear but you don't agree with them.*
As broad as it is long.	*Something which is the same one way as it is another / you will get the same result whichever way you do something.*
So near but yet so far.	*Something was quite close to the target but it missed and in the context of things it's actually relatively far away.*
That's the Real McCoy.	*The genuine person or thing.*
Both yer friend an' yer enemy think that ye'll never die.	*Your friend thinks that you will always be there for them and your enemy can't wait until you die.*
That's a whole new ball game.	*That is a completely different situation.*
The most important things in life aren't things.	*Things like love and happiness are not physical things which can be seen or bought but without them you would sad.*
Don't fly in the face of God.	*To go against accepted wisdom, knowledge or common practice.*

I cried because I had no shoes 'til I met the man with no feet.

Don't get upset about your problems because there is usually someone who is a lot worse than you.

Beat fair and square.

To have been beat at something legally and honestly.

Born with a silver spoon in one's mouth.

Born into affluence. Unlike ordinary children, that is, who have to wait until their christening before they receive the traditional gift of a silver spoon from their godparents.

It swings in roundabouts.

Everything always goes back to what it was before. There are as many advantages to a situation as there are disadvantages.

I'm workin' on borrowed time.

My time has run out and I will get in trouble soon or I am not expected to live much longer.

They're over the moon.

They are so happy or overjoyed by something that has happened to them.

The bigger the better.

The bigger something is the better it will be.

The more the merrier.

The more people who attend an event, the better it will be.

It's written all over his face.	*The expression on someone's face that shows their true feelings or thoughts.*
I've drawn the short straw.	*I am member of a group and I have been given an unpleasant job.*
Fish always stink from the head down.	*This means many organisations always fail from at the top due to poor management.*
My hands are tied.	*I cannot do anything because I am not allowed or there is a law / rule preventing me from doing it.*
I've bigger fish to fry.	*I have something which more important to attend to.*
Stick it up yer jumper.	*To inform someone that they can do whatever they like with an object.*
I believe ye, thousands wouldn't.	*I believe you are telling the truth while many others wouldn't.*
Keep me in the picture.	*Keep me informed about the situation.*
I wouldn't do that for all the tea in China.	*I wouldn't do that no matter how much I was being offered.*
You're fightin' a losin' battle.	*You are trying to very hard to do something but you will never succeed.*

185

Watch this space.	*To imply that you think there will be exciting things in the future.*
I've hit rock bottom.	*I have hit my lowest level.*
Birds of a feather flock together.	*People with similar characteristics or interests will often choose to spend time together.*
One man's rubbish is another man's treasure / one man's meat is another man's poison.	*Different people have different tastes.*
May ye be half an hour in heaven before the Devil even knows that you're dead.	*You would like someone to go straight to heaven and not hell.*
The best thing since sliced bread.	*Something which is extremely good.*
Keep yer friends close but yer enemies closer.	*Watch your enemies more than your friends.*
Too many irons in the fire.	*Trying to do too many things at once.*
Ye'll have to spill the beans.	*You will have to reveal information to others.*
Ye may tread lightly.	*Be careful.*
Be careful who ye walk on, on the way down because ye might meet them on the way back down.	*You should be careful not to annoy or offend anyone as you work your way up in an organisation as it could go wrong and you might them.*

Famous Sayings throughout the world

Bad news travels fast.	*If something serious has happened to someone many people will find out about it quickly.*
A family that prays together stays together.	*A family that shares values and interests are more likely to stay together.*
There's no place like home.	*No matter how far you travel in life, you will always be welcomed and comforted in that little corner of the world you call home.*
Fail to prepare, prepare to fail.	*If you don't prepare for whatever you want to do in life, it could all go wrong for you and you could fail.*
That'll take the wind out of his sails.	*That will make him feel less confident or less determined to do by doing something they were not expecting.*
Patience is a virtue that causes no shame.	*It is a great asset to have patience.*
Ye have to read between the lines.	*To detect an obscure or unexplained meaning.*
A rollin' stone gathers no moss.	*Someone who is always on the move and who doesn't stay in one place for very long do not pick up any responsibilities.*

April fool's dead an' gone an' you're the fool for carryin' it on.	*April fool's day traditionally only lasts until 12.00 am, but if someone carries it on past this time then people use this.*
It's goin' to go down to the wire.	*A closely fought competition which will be decided by the narrowest of margins.*
Ye win some, ye lose some.	*You will win some games and you will lose some, you just have to accept this.*
Too little, too late.	*There was not enough help given to save a situation or it wasn't given soon enough.*
Like father like son.	*A son will always resemble his father in the way they do and say things.*
One good turn deserves another.	*If someone does you a favour then you should do them a favour in return.*
Ye live an' learn.	*As you go through life, you learn more new things and you become more experienced.*
Out of sight, out of mind.	*If you don't see someone or something then you are more likely to forget about them.*
Ye have to crawl before ye can walk.	*You have to learn something progressively and develop as you go along.*

No pain, no gain	*You cannot achieve real success at anything without great effort and sacrifice.*
Nobody is perfect.	*Everyone has their faults and failings and every human being makes mistakes.*
It's always been survival of the fittest.	*Those who are best suited or most skilled will be better equipped to carry out their jobs or life in general.*
A bad tradesman blames his tools.	*A person who is bad at their job will refuse to take responsibility for it and instead blame the tools they are using.*
It's best to forgive an' forget.	*It is better to forgive someone for something they have done to you.*
Never judge a book by its cover.	*Don't make little of someone just because of the way they look.*
That's just the icin' on the cake.	*Something good that is added to another good thing or an extra enhancement.*
Hunger is the best sauce.	*When you are hungry, everything tastes good.*
Tip of the iceberg.	*When something happens that is small in comparison to what is about to happen or has happened.*

Famous last words.

A prediction which is likely to be proved wrong in the future.

Every picture tells a story.

Used when what has really happened in a situation is clear because of the way someone or something looks.

Nero fiddled while Rome burnt.

To occupy yourself with unimportant things while neglecting serious other things during a crisis.

A picture is worth a thousand words.

Refers to the fact that a complex description can be explained with a simple image.

A problem shared is a problem solved / halved.

When you tell someone about a problem, it makes it easier for you.

Actions speak louder than words.

What someone does is more important than what someone says they will do.

All's well that ends well.

A satisfactory conclusion makes up for earlier disappointment.

Beggars can't be choosers.

Someone has to accept what is available in difficult circumstances.

Honestly's the best policy.

You should always be honest even if you have done something wrong.

The tallest flowers hide the strongest nettles.	*People in high places have the worst faults.*
Seein' is believin'.	*You will only believe something is true when you see it for yourself.*
The apple never falls far from the tree.	*A family member who does move far from the family home where they were brought up.*
Two's company, but three's a crowd.	*Two people are relaxed and enjoy each other's company but when another person joins them it makes them feel less comfortable.*
When in Rome, do as the Romans do.	*When you are visiting a new place, you should try to do as the local people.*
While there's life, there's hope.	*When someone is still living no matter how sick they are, at least there is still hope of them surviving.*
A flower blooms more than once.	*If you happen to miss an occasion, you can avail of it another time.*
A tree is known by its fruit.	*You can tell what family a person belongs to by how they look or act.*
Charity begins at home.	*Be generous to your own family before you offer help to others.*

Where there's a will, there's a way.	*If you are determined, you can find a way to achieve what you want no matter how difficult it may be.*
A stumble may prevent a fall.	*A minor incident may prevent a major incident from happening.*
Aim for the stars and ye might hit the moon.	*You should begin with high ambitions and you might get lucky some day.*
Expect the unexpected.	*You should be prepared for anything as you never know what could happen in life.*
It's not over 'til the fat lady sings.	*Someone is losing a game but there is still time left and there is a possibility that they could beat their opponents.*
There's a lesson to be learnt.	*Something that happens which demonstrates how something should be done.*
The grace of God is found between the saddle an' the ground.	*It is up to God what happens to you when you have an accident.*
A friend's eye is a good mirror.	*A friend will always tell you the truth whenever you ask them a question.*
Desperate times call for desperate measures.	*When people get into trouble they may be forced to do things which they wouldn't normally do.*

If ye can't beat them, join them.	*If you have been fighting against a group who you cannot win against, you should give up and join them.*
If you're not in ye can't win.	*If you don't take part in a competition or put your name forward for something then you cannot win it.*
Practice makes perfect.	*If you continually practice something then eventually you will become perfect at it.*
Better late than never.	*It's better to arrive late to something than not to arrive at all.*
Less is more.	*Sometimes the less things you have the better it looks and by paying attention to detail people will appreciate it more.*
Far away fields seem green.	*People are always under the impression that there are more opportunities for them overseas.*
That's music to my ears.	*News which someone is pleased to hear.*
Great minds think alike.	*Very intelligent people tend to come up with the same ideas.*
An apple a day keeps the doctor away.	*Apples are said to promote good health so if you eat them every day it will reduce the chances of you becoming ill.*

Good things come in small packages.

People will say this to emphasize the fact that something does not need to be big in order to be good.

Speed and accuracy do not agree.

You cannot do something at speed and still be accurate.

Blood is thicker than water.

People always tend to trust a member of their family before they would trust someone who is not related to them.

It takes two to tango.

Something you say which means if two people were involved in a bad situation, both must be responsible.

I'm goin' to throw in the towel / throw down the sponge.

To give up or surrender something.

Leave no stone unturned.

To search everywhere for something and try everything you can think of.

Mums are like buttons, they hold things together.

Everyone relies on their mothers to do things for them and they are always there for you when you need them.

An eye for an eye.

Retaliation in the same form as the offence provoking it.

What's born in the blood comes out in the flesh.

Whatever qualities a father or mother has, their offspring will have as well.

Be-all and end-all.	*An essential element or the entire purpose of something.*
Burnin' the candle at both ends.	*Someone who is worn out due to work commitments or socialising.*
There's no smoke without fire.	*When people suspect something; there is usually a good reason for the suspicion.*
You're only rubbin' salt into the wounds.	*To make a bad experience / situation even worse.*
A lie travels further than the truth.	*People are more than likely to remember a lie than the truth.*
Go back to the drawin' board.	*You are trying to complete a task then you have to start over again.*
Break a leg.	*A well-known saying in theatre meaning 'good-luck'.*
The truth hurts.	*People don't like to hear the truth because they know they have done wrong.*
Once seen never forgotten.	*Whenever you see someone who like or dislike you will not forget them.*
Fight fire with fire.	*To combat one evil thing by doing another evil thing.*
If ye something done always ask a busy person.	*A busy person is more likely to do something for you than a lazy person.*

Good fences make good neighbours.	*This phrase means it is better to mind your own business and respect the privacy of others.*
Home is where the heart is.	*Your true home is with the person or in the place you love the most in the world.*
Gone but not forgotten.	*Someone who has just died or has moved away and who people will always remember.*
Three things come without askin' fear, jealousy and love.	*These things all come to us and we have no control over these emotions.*
Put that in yer pipe an' smoke it.	*Someone has to accept what you have just said whether they like it or not.*
Beauty's only skin deep.	*Being beautiful only counts for your physical appearance.*
All good things come to those who wait.	*A phrase to emphasise the importance of having patience.*
The cracks are startin' to show.	*It is becoming clear that a person or an organisation can no longer cope.*
Ye only live once.	*Try to do everything you can because you only have one life.*
It's not a fish 'til ye have it on the bank.	*Don't count on it until you have it.*

Chapter 14

Wise Craics

Fences / walls have ears

Let sleepin' dogs lie.	*When something has been working well for a while you should leave it alone.*
Ye can't transplant an old tree.	*It's difficult to move something or someone who has been in the same place for a long time.*
The early bird gets the worm.	*If you get up early in the mornings then you will succeed.*
It's the quiet pigs who get the grain.	*It is those who are quiet that you don't expect who actually get more than others.*
Barkin' dogs seldom bite.	*People who talk a lot or threaten are not harmful.*
Ye can't make a silk purse out of a sow's ear.	*You can't make a high quality product using bad materials.*
Manners are easily carried / manners are free / manners don't cost anythin'.	*Good manners are essential.*
Ye either have it or ye don't an' you don't!	*You are either good at something or you are not.*
If ye never have it, ye never miss it.	*You won't miss what you never had.*
If ye do have it, ye never lose it.	*If you are naturally good at something you always will be.*
Ye can't teach yer grandmother to suck eggs.	*Don't instruct an experienced person.*

A bad apple can rot the whole cart.

One bad individual can make the others around them seem bad as well.

Fences / walls have ears.

Be careful what you say because you never know who may be listening.

If ye believed all ye were told, you'd never get outa bed.

If you believed everything you hear you would do nothing.

Measure twice cut once.

Always measure something twice before cutting it.

Even a small thorn can cause festerin'.

A small problem can turn into a bigger one.

Take yer points an' yer goals will come.

Be patient, a goal opportunity will come eventually.

Ye never miss the water 'til the well runs dry.

You're not grateful for what you have until you lose it.

It's the squeaky wheel that gets the grease.

A disabled or less fortunate person will always get more benefits than an able person due to their disadvantage.

No news is good news.

If you don't hear any news at all this is a good thing because at least it is not bad news.

Don't bring one with ye because there'll be one there when ye get.

Don't bring a person who has a tendency to mess around to a venue because there will be plenty of people misbehaving there.

Least said is the easiest mended.	*A bad event can be forgotten easily if you don't mention it.*
Practice what ye preach.	*You should do what you tell others to do.*
Ye never know what's 'round the corner.	*You do not know what will happen next in your life.*
The best advice is found on the pillow.	*It's not good to worry about your problems immediately it's better to solve the problem after a good night's sleep.*
If ye were to work for nothin' ye'd never be idle.	*If you did everything free of charge you would always be employed.*
It's no use cryin' over spilt milk.	*There is no point in worrying about something which has already happened.*
A narrow neck, keeps the bottle from bein' emptied in one swig.	*If you can only get a small amount at a time then you cannot take it all at once.*
A kettle never boiled without fire.	*Energy is needed to make anything happen.*
One egg today is better than two tomorrow.	*Possession is better than promises.*
Don't speak too soon.	*Don't say anything because you can never be sure how it will work out.*
Wait a minute to study the form.	*Consider the situation before you make.*

Ye'll know for again.

You have learnt from a mistake and you will not make again in the future.

Show me yer company an' I'll tell ye what you're like.

You can judge a person by the company they keep.

God has funny ways of workin'.

People say that god may make life hard for you if you have done something wrong.

If I only knew then what I know now.

If you had known something in the past which you know now then you would have made better decisions.

Leave it to 'til dust settles a bit.

Do nothing at present until people have calmed down again.

At least he has his foot in the door anyway.

He has made himself known and has a chance of getting a job.

It's bad but it could be worse.

Something may seem terrible at first but when you think about it, and then it could have been much worse.

Ye need to look after number one.

You should always make sure to look after yourself.

What doesn't break ye will make ye.

If you survive something you will only benefit from it.

Never dread the winter 'til the snow is on the blanket.

Don't dread something until it has actually arrived and is directly affecting you.

Look after the pennies an' the pounds will look after themselves.

If you look after small sums of money then it will accumulate over time.

Ye have to speculate to accumulate.

You have to spend money to earn money.

Two heads are better than one.

It means it is better to work in a group than by yourself.

The cream will always come to the top.

The heroic or intelligent among the population will always rise above the stupid or less skilled individuals.

Think before ye speak.

Think carefully about what you are going to say before you say anything.

Rome wasn't built in a day.

It takes a long time to build something.

Too many chiefs and not enough Indians.

There are too many managers and not enough workers to work efficiently.

Don't cut off yer nose to spite yer face.

To do something because you are angry even if it will get you into trouble.

Half a loaf's better than no bread.

It is better to have something even if it is very little rather than having nothing at all.

People in glass houses shouldn't throw stones.

You should not criticize other people for their bad qualities if you have them yourself.

A moment on the lips is a lifetime on the hips.

It is easy to eat nice food which you enjoy, but excess fat is hard to get off again.

Take every day as it comes.

Don't plan too far ahead.

Ye don't know what ye have 'til it's gone.

You don't realise how important something or someone was until it's taken from you.

Nothin' is a problem unless it's yer health.

People become stressed over minor problems but major problems is your health.

Sow in the spring, reap in the autumn.

You cannot expect to reap the benefits of something if you do not prepare for it in advance.

We may just leave it in God's hands.

You believe in fate and will just wait to see what happens.

See no evil, hear no evil, an' speak no evil.

If you are not exposed to bad things, you are unlikely to be involved in it.

It'd be easier to put a camel through the eye of a needle.

A task which would be impossible to complete.

The proof of the puddin' is in the eatin'.

The quality of something is not certain until it is tested directly.

The more things change, the more they stay the same.

If you continually keep changing the way someone does something they will just continue to do things the way they always did.

Better alone than in bad company.	*If you are alone then you are less likely to get into trouble.*
Easier said than done.	*Sounds good in theory, less so in practice.*
That's water under the bridge now.	*Something which is in the past and people have forgotten about.*
It takes a wise man to act a fool.	*Someone who lets on to be foolish but they actually know exactly what they are doing.*
You're only addin' fuel to the fire.	*You are making a situation worse.*
When the apple is ripe, it will fall.	*Things will only happen when they are ready to happen.*

Tips for the future

Never look a gift horse in the mouth.	*Always be grateful to be given something.*
Ye only get out of it, what ye put into it.	*If you don't make an effort you won't reap the benefits.*
Everythin' happens for a reason.	*When something happened which might seem bad at the time, but in the long term it might have stopped a catastrophic thing happening.*
Ye have to take the good with the bad.	*In life you must accept that some good and bad things will happen to you.*

Ye don't know who's watchin' ye.	*Other people may be observing what you do.*
It's the quiet one's ye wanta watch.	*Implies that quiet people tend to be sneaky.*
Always take people as ye find them.	*Accept people as they are.*
Live everyday as if it were yer last.	*You should value every moment of your life, and use your time on earth wisely.*
Ye need to see the bigger picture.	*You need to take an overview.*
The less said the better / the easier mended.	*Something should not be talked about any further.*
If ye want somethin' done right then ye should do it yourself.	*You could do a job better yourself than anyone else could.*
It's better lookin' at them than lookin' for them.	*It is better to have too much than not enough.*
You're a long time dead.	*You should live life to the full, because you will not live forever.*
The mill can't grind with water that has past.	*It is impossible to fix things that are past.*
Never put off 'til tomorrow, what ye can do today.	*Always do things when you have the opportunity to do them and don't put things off until another time.*

Stick to yer guns.	*To stand up yourself and remain firm to what you believe in.*
There's no point in beatin' around the bush.	*Stop wasting time or trying to avoid a question.*
No matter how long the day, night comes.	*It may seem like a really long day but you can be rest assured evening will come.*
An inch is as good as a mile.	*If something moves even a little it may be make a huge difference.*
Don't put new wine into old bottles.	*You should not try to combine new things with old things.*
He who fights, an' runs away, lives to fight another day.	*If you don't stay to the end of a fight you will survive.*
Let nature take its course.	*To allow something to happen naturally.*
One door closes another opens.	*Anyone who loses a job or opportunity will have more opportunities in the future.*
A change is as good as a rest.	*You get as much good from changing the work you do as you would from a rest.*
The older ye are, the wiser ye get.	*As you get older you are able to make better decisions.*
All good things have to come to an end.	*Good things don't last forever and usually not as long as people would like them to.*

Look at everythin' as if it was the first an' last time ye were seein' it.

Always pay good attention to something when you see it.

Take it on the chin.

You just have to accept something and move on as it can't be changed.

What goes in must come out.

If something has gone in before then it will come out again.

It's never too late to learn somethin'.

You can start to learn to do something new at any age.

Self praise is no recognition.

If you praise yourself, people will think that you are boastful and not respect you.

Don't bite off more than ye can chew.

Do not attempt to do more than you are capable of.

The man that made time made plenty of time.

Used whenever someone says that they do not have time to do anything.

Stick to what ye know.

Only do something which you have a good knowledge of.

There is no time like the present.

You should do things now rather than leaving them until another time.

Ye can't have yer cake an' eat it.

You can't consume something whilst preserving it as well.

All good things come to those who wait.

Waiting patiently is the best way to get what you want.

Ye can't win them all.	*It would be impossible to be successful at everything you do.*
Whatever doesn't kill us makes us stronger.	*If you try something and it doesn't do you any harm then it will only give you more confidence in the future.*
You're only young once.	*Do as many things as you can when you are young because when you grow old, you may not be able to.*
Things aren't always as they seem.	*Something may seem good in a picture but in reality it might not be good at all.*
The less ye know the better.	*A way of indicating that you think something should not be talked about any further.*
You're not 'ere for a long time you're only 'ere for a good time.	*Live your life to the full, do as much as you can because you won't be alive for very long.*
It's not what ye know it's who ye know / 'I'm in the know!'	*Knowing someone in authority is helpful.*
Ye shouldn't tempt fate.	*To provoke or risk something that could go seriously wrong.*
Say nothin' 'til ye hear more.	*Don't say anything until the position becomes clear.*
Always be on the safe side.	*To be well prepared in case something could go wrong.*

It's all a learnin' curve

You learn things as you go along and from your mistakes.

Don't cross yer bridges before ye come to 'em.

Don't worry about something until it actually happens.

Health is yer wealth.

A clean bill of health is the most important thing, even more than being wealthy.

Ye can't live on last week's dinner.

You must continue to earn money.

It's better to be a coward for a minute than to be dead for the rest of yer life.

It is safer to act like a coward and be embarrassed than to be killed doing something.

Ye should keep yer ear to the ground.

You should keep me well informed about something.

Look before ye leap.

Don't do something without careful consideration beforehand.

Ye should always aim high.

Try to be ambitious and set yourself a challenging goal to achieve.

Never bite the hands that feed ye.

Don't criticize the person or organisation that helps you or pays your wages.

Pen an' paper reuses nothin'.

You could write anything down and people would believe it.

A job worth doin' is worth doin' well.

Always try to do everything to the best of your ability.

Chapter 15
Compliments

He is a very level headed person

She's as quiet as a mouse.	*She is a very quiet individual.*
A heart like a lion.	*Very brave.*
They're not just a one trick pony.	*They are multi-talented.*
He has eyes on him like a travellin' rat.	*He has got excellent eyesight.*
They can swim like a fish.	*They are excellent swimmers.*
Ye wouldn't know that they were in the house or ye wouldn't hear their word.	*They are very quiet.*
He can go like a stag.	*He can move at a great speed.*
They'll bounce back from it alright.	*They will recover quickly after a setback.*
There's not a bad bone in 'er body.	*She is a good person.*
Ye wouldn't hear a peep outa 'em.	*They wouldn't make the slightest sound.*
He has brains to burn.	*He is very intelligent.*
They wouldn't harm a fly.	*They wouldn't hurt anything.*
He's very level headed.	*He is sensible.*
Ye should take a leaf outa his book.	*You should copy something which he has done.*
They're easy on the eye.	*They are good looking.*

She's come outa 'er shell.	*She has stopped being shy.*
He won at a canter.	*He won easily.*
What ye see is what ye get with them.	*There is nothing hidden whatever you see is exactly as it is.*
Ye couldn't hold a candle to 'em.	*You couldn't compete with them.*
There's a method in his madness.	*He is being sensible.*
He's as cool as ice.	*He is cool, calm and collected.*
A face without freckles is like a sky without stars.	*Freckles are attractive.*
They'd go to the end of the earth for ye.	*Those who would go to extreme lengths to help you in whatever way they could.*
I have to take ma hat off to ye.	*I admire what you have done.*
A handsome woman's easily dressed.	*A beautiful or good looking person always looks lovely no matter how they are dressed.*
He has a whole lot of strings til' his bow.	*He is involved in many different things or has many different ways to make a living.*
Ye wouldn't hear a mute outa 'em.	*You wouldn't hear them make a sound.*

He could keep a nation goin' or keep a house goin'.	*He makes everyone laugh.*
She's so quiet she knocks on the door with a sponge.	*She is very quiet.*
You've the gift of the gab.	*The ability to speak easily and confidently in a way that makes people want to listen to you.*
They'd kill ye with kindness.	*They will be very nice to you.*
Ye could turn yer hand to anythin'.	*You could do anything.*
They'd do anythin' for ye at the drop of a hat.	*They are very obliging.*
He's made of strong stuff.	*He made a quick recovery.*
They've the patience of a saint.	*They are very patient.*
You're worth yer weight in gold.	*You are very useful or helpful.*
The children were as good as gold.	*The children were well behaved.*
She's a tarbil dacent woman.	*A kind and helpful woman.*
They get on like a house on fire.	*Two people who enjoy each other's company.*
I'm always singin' yer praises.	*I am always praising you.*
He was a right ole spud.	*He was a good guy.*

They're a breathe of fresh air.	*They are enthusiastic and happy go lucky people.*
She's just like a wee doll.	*She is dainty.*
You've got yer head screwed on anyway.	*You are a wise person.*
Yer a whole good 'an.	*You are a wonderful individual.*
She's a heart of corn.	*She is a kind and caring woman.*
He's a civil auld craithur.	*He is an easy going man and is nice to others.*
Ye wouldn't hear 'er word.	*An individual who is softy spoken or rarely ever speaks.*
They'd go to hell an' back for ye.	*They would do anything for you.*
He does everythin' by the book.	*He is a very honest person.*
They could hear the grass growin'.	*They have very good hearing.*
He never even broke sweat.	*He can complete a task with ease.*
She'd give ye the bite outa 'er mouth.	*She is an extremely generous person.*
He'd never pass ye.	*He always acknowledges you.*

Chapter 16

Funny Auld Sayings

The house is that cold ye could chill beef in it

It would stick to ye like shite til' a blanket.	*Something or someone that would be hard to get rid of.*
Ye must be scrappin' the arse of the barrel with that.	*You haven't much left and you are using something that is of poor quality.*
The house is that cold that ye could chill beef in it.	*A house which is extremely cold.*
Let us out but don't leave us.	*People that need to be monitored closely because they get up to mischief.*
He farts that much that he'd need corked.	*Someone who constantly passes wind.*
Ye'd think that they were catchin' flies.	*A person who has their mouth open wide.*
Those pair could live in yer ear.	*People who spend all of their time at your house.*
Ye wouldn't know yer luck 'til ye look at the tail of yer shirt.	*You don't know how lucky you are until you look at the end of your shirt to see if you have shit yourself.*
They'll be fallin' over each other to get in the door.	*When people are giving out things for free everyone will be in a hurry to get some for themselves.*
He couldn't play with himself never mind anyone else.	*He is no use at playing anything.*
A policeman wouldn't ask ye that!	*You should not have asked that question.*

Yer bedroom is like the pits.	*Your bedroom which is very dirty and untidy.*
Never eat yellow snow!	*Snow turns yellow when it's been urinated on and that's you shouldn't eat it.*
The only good thing to come outa that place is the road outa it.	*This implies that there is nothing good in a particular location.*
Right be good an' if ye can't be good be safe / careful!	*If you're not going to behave then make sure you're safe.*
Don't do anythin' I wouldn't do, although that doesn't rule out much.	*I would do anything.*
That dinner wouldn't fill a hole in yer tooth.	*A small dinner which you don't feel full after eating.*
Ye might as well put it in the newspaper / put it on the news when ye tell them.	*A particular person would tell everyone if you told them something.*
He'd work the shirt off his back.	*He works extremely hard and rarely takes a break.*
I could have soaped ma arse an' slid the whole way from Belfast to Dublin in the time it took to do that.	*Something which took a long time to complete.*
It's the real dog's balls.	*The best of the best or the absolute apex.*
There's not a fart in this town they don't know about!	*They know everything about in an area.*

If ye were any slower ye'd be stopped or ye'd be dead.

Describes the person that is extremely slow.

It's as scarce as shite from a rockin' horse.

Something which does not exist.

He'd steal the sugar outa yer tea.

He would stop at nothing to steal from you.

I'm as sick as the plane goin' to Lourdes.

I feel really ill.

If he went to a weddin' he'd stay for the christenin'.

He has a reputation for overstaying their welcome.

If she fell in shite, she'd come out smellin' out of roses.

She tends to be lucky because no manner what happens to them they always seem to be ok.

I'm that hungry, I'd eat the picture of the last supper.

I am starving with hunger.

Don't get yer knickers in a twist.

Don't get flustered / annoyed because things will be ok.

You're well travelled, from the bedroom to the kitchen.

Usually said to someone who is overweight.

She thinks that 'er shit doesn't stink.

She thinks she is better than anyone else.

One eye lookin' at ye an' one eye lookin' for ye.

A cross-eyed person.

It's alright actin' the tin pig 'til someone gets dinged.

It is ok messing around until someone gets badly hurt.

It's alright messin' about 'til someone loses an eye.

People think that it is fine to be messing around but something could go wrong.

Take him outa the town an' he's lost.

Those who know how to navigate their way around the town, but, if you take them out of it they would be lost.

He only hears what he wants to hear.

He lets on that he does not hear certain things because it's not something he wants to hear.

That referee's eyes must be in his arse.

A referee who didn't see an incident during a football match and it was blatantly obvious.

They've nothin' to do an' all day to do it.

They don't work and sit around the house all day.

Have ye no home to go til'!

Those who stay at someone's house longer than their welcome.

Beauty is only a light switch away.

If you don't find the your partner just turn the light off because then you don't see them.

There's no use in carryin' an umbrella if yer shoes are leakin'.

There is no point in doing something if it's going to happen anyway.

You're not a bad child. When you're sleepin'.

You are only well behaved is when you are sleeping.

My mouth is that dry I could suck moisture off a cow's arse through a hedge.

I am thirsty and I would do anything for a drink.

I wouldn't say anythin' to 'er because she'd ate the face off ye.

She would get cross and shout at me if I said anything to her.

The softest part of him is his teeth.

He lets on that he does not know much but in actual fact he does.

I know ye might look like a cabbage but you're not that green.

Even though you might look stupid you are actually quite smart.

Accidents can happen, even in bed.

You could have an accident in bed and your wife or girlfriend could get pregnant.

If ye don't care, ye may buy a pram.

If you don't care about getting pregnant then you can expect to have a baby.

They couldn't hold their water.

When people are told a piece of information and they were unable to keep it a secret but instead they tell everyone.

That'll learn ye to keep yer mouth shut.

You said something which meant that you got hurt.

They have more connections than BT.

They know many different people throughout the country.

Would ye like some tea with that milk?

Tea which has an awful lot of milk in it and very little tea.

Ye can't hold what ye haven't got in yer hand.

If a person passes wind they will say this because it means that they couldn't help it.

Where ye born in a field?

Said to those who don't close doors behind when entering or leaving a room.

She's that quiet that ye'd think if ye said boo to 'er that she'd cry.

A person who looks as if they are scared all the time.

There's no point in takin' sand to the beach.

Don't take your partner to a party because then you can't get out with anyone else.

I wouldn't go to see them playin' if they were in the back garden.

I really don't like that band or football team and I wouldn't go to see them playing regardless of how close they were.

Ye wouldn't make a great window.

Usually said to someone when they are blocking your view.

I know you're a pane but not a see through one.

I can not see through you.

People think that the sun shines out of his arse.

To love and admire someone so much that you do not think they have any bad qualities.

They'd give ye the shites.

They really get on your nerves.

If you'd open yer eyes you'd see more.

You are not observant.

Somebody dropped one.

Someone has farted.

You keep talkin' an' I'll keep sholvin'.	*Someone is talking shite or speaking about something that makes absolutely nonsense.*
I'm goin' out for Halloween can I borrow yer face?	*To imply that someone has an ugly or scary face.*
Half the country knows me an' the other half wants to know me.	*Basically, saying that most people know you and if they don't know you they want to get to know you.*
He wouldn't sleep in the same house as a shovel standin' up.	*He doesn't like to do any manual labour.*
Home was never like this.	*Usually said to someone who wants to leave a party to go home.*
He has a hump on him like a dog shittin' on a razor blade.	*He has a hump on his back.*
He hasn't a snowball's chance in hell.	*An individual that you believe to have no hope of doing something.*
Shut yer mouth an' eat yer dinner.	*Stop talking and eat your dinner.*
Ye may go for a clean pair of pants after that.	*That was so scary you could have shit yourself.*
Bob's yer uncle an' fanny's yer aunt.	*Good that's something finished with.*
You're talkin' outa yer arse.	*You are talking nonsense.*

The crows won't shite on them for a day or two.	*They are due to spend a long time in prison.*
They were up an' down like a whore's knickers.	*Anything which is constantly going up and down.*
Who cut yer hair? The council?	*Used to make fun of someone's hairstyle.*
Yer face looks like a bulldog lickin' piss off a nettle.	*Your face doesn't look particularly happy.*
There's no point shuttin' the stable door when the horse is away.	*There is no point locking up your processions after you have been robbed.*
His feet are that big that he'll soon have to pay road tax for 'em.	*He has oversized feet.*
Yer hair is that long, ye could wipe yer arse with it.	*Your hair is very long.*
They're that nosy that they would ask ye when ye shit last.	*They would ask you very personal questions.*
Ye may wipe yer mouth because there's shite all 'round it.	*Said to someone who you don't believe what they are saying.*
If it wasn't for bad luck I'd have none.	*Those with very poor luck.*
They'd tell ye horse shite was lemon.	*They are compulsive liars.*

No matter where ye are in the place they will be beside ye.

An extremely large or obese person.

The quickest way to double yer money is to fold it in half an' put it back in yer pocket.

You shouldn't gamble because you only end up losing money.

Make sure ye put that paint on the right way.

It doesn't matter what way you apply the paint because it is liquid and doesn't have a front or back.

They could run their house on shoe string.

They are very good at managing their money.

He would put plenty of sugar 'round yer lips but he wouldn't give ye any.

Those who praise you a lot but they wouldn't give you anything for what you did.

I have got more stitches than an Armani suit.

I needed a large number of stitches in my wound.

So you are gettin' married then I suppose ye can't be happy all yer life.

People will say this to you when you are getting married to say that you won't be happy anymore.

As weak as holy water in an orange hall.

A transparent liquid or an alcohol with little volume in it.